With all good wishes
from the Staff of S.P.C.K.

Christmas 1964

Canterbury
Essays and Addresses

Canterbury
Essays and Addresses

Michael Ramsey
Archbishop of Canterbury

LONDON

S·P·C·K

1964

First published in 1964
by S.P.C.K.
Holy Trinity Church
Marylebone Road
London N.W.1
Printed and bound in Great Britain
by Hazell Watson & Viney Ltd
Aylesbury, Bucks

Preface

The essays and addresses in this book belong to the period since I became Archbishop of Canterbury in June 1961, with the exception of the lecture on Heaven and Hell, three of the biographical essays, and two of the pastoral addresses, which belongs to my time at York. The reader is asked to forgive a little repetition due to the "occasional" character of the contents of the book; but he will find, I hope, an underlying coherence of theme concerning the nature of the Christian faith and its bearing upon the life of the world.

If the biographical studies may seem to stand a little apart from the rest of the volume, I believe that the six Anglican divines who are recalled can assist our understanding of a great tradition which is able to serve the unity of Christendom and the presentation of a supernatural faith to contemporary society.

Easter 1964   MICHAEL CANTUAR:

Contents

Preface   5

THEOLOGY

The Crisis of Human Freedom   11
The Waley Cohen Lecture, 4 December 1962

Christian Spirituality and the Modern World   20
A Lecture to the Cercle Oecuménique in the University of Louvain,
3 May 1963

Heaven and Hell   32
The Drew Lecture, New College, London, 25 November 1960

Christianity and the Supernatural   41
The Ethel M. Wood Lecture, 5 March 1963

UNITY

Unity, Holiness, and Truth   55
An Address to the Assembly of the World Council of Churches in New
Delhi, November 1961

Constantinople and Canterbury   60
A Lecture to the University of Athens, 7 May 1962

Anglicans and the Future   74
A Sermon at the Opening Service of the Anglican Congress, Toronto,
13 August 1963

THE CONTEMPORARY WORLD

Christian Responsibility in a World Society   83
An Address in London, 15 November 1962

Sex and Civilization   87
An Article in the *Sunday Times*, 17 February 1963

The Laws of Divorce   92
A Speech on the Committee Stage of the Matrimonial Causes and
Reconciliation Bill in the House of Lords, 21 June 1963

The Robbins Report   97
A Speech in the House of Lords, 11 December 1963

In Memory of President Kennedy   101
An Address in St Paul's Cathedral, 1 December 1963

BIOGRAPHY

Charles Simeon: Evangelical and Churchman
An Article in *The Church of England Newspaper*, March 1959
107

Dean Church and the Growth of Anglicanism
An Article in *The York Quarterly*, August 1958
112

Herbert Hensley Henson
A Sermon preached in the Chapel of All Souls College, Oxford, 16 June 1963
116

Lionel Thornton: Theologian
An Article in *C.R.*, Lady Day 1961
127

Herbert Kelly: Prophet
An Address in Manchester for the Centenary of his Birth, 28 June 1960
133

George Bell
An Address in Chichester Cathedral, 4 November 1961
140

PASTORALIA

Retreats: Their Aim and Conduct
Based upon Addresses at Wydale Hall, Yorkshire, in 1958 and at Oxford in 1962
145

The Monastic Life
A Sermon at the Consecration of the new Chapel of the Order of the Holy Paraclete at St Hilda's Priory, Whitby, 3 May 1957
153

The Priest
A Sermon at the Cuddesdon Festival, 1958
156

The Bishop
A Sermon at the Installation of the Bishop of Washington in the Cathedral of St Peter and St Paul, Washington, 1 November 1962
161

Whose Hearts God has Touched
A Sermon at the Enthronement in Canterbury Cathedral, 27 June 1961
165

THEOLOGY

The Crisis of Human Freedom

Amongst the memories of my very young school days is the occasion when the familiar essay was set: "Would you have been a Cavalier or a Roundhead and why?". I wrote: "I would have been a Roundhead because the Roundheads were more tolerant than the Cavaliers", and the master wrote in red ink in the margin "I doubt this". It is, of course, all more complex than any little boy could realize, but perhaps it is not incongruous that a little boy who at any rate picked tolerance as the criterion for his approval should, half a century later, be giving the Waley Cohen lecture with Tolerance and Freedom as his theme. I want to speak about some of the difficulties with which Tolerance and Freedom have been beset, and about the critical condition of both of them to-day.

Was the master right or was I? No doubt the Cromwellians gave signal service to the growth of toleration. No single act of toleration has been more important or creative than Cromwell's own restoration of the Jews. But how complex was the struggle, and how complex is the award of prizes to this side or that. Milton in his *Areopagitica* argued that persecution was unnecessary for the preservation of truth and a hindrance to the propagation of the truth: yet even he would allow no toleration for Roman Catholics. Jeremy Taylor's *Liberty of Prophesying* was a high churchman's plea for liberty of speech against the restrictions imposed by the Puritan Long Parliament. The Pilgrim Fathers left our shores in the quest of a land where they could organize toleration for themselves, and their feeling for toleration was ahead of their time. Yet, once beyond the Atlantic, what limitations there were; states became theocracies each with its theological system, often intolerant of all others. To Maryland belongs the honour of proclaiming in its Charter equal toleration to every and any person professing belief in Jesus Christ. On both sides of the Atlantic toleration grew, as Bishop Creighton argued in his Hulsean Lectures on *Persecution and Tolerance*, far less through any convinced theory as to why toleration was right than through the sheer empirical necessity of groups in politics and religion to allow others to survive if they were to survive themselves. So the impetus ran on; in England the nineteenth century completed what the eighteenth century began: Jews, Roman Catholics, Dissenters, Atheists were allowed to exist, allowed the franchise, and allowed access to academic equality and honour.

But what is toleration? Toleration means that a man who holds opinions does not want to impose them on others by any external pressure or enforce them by any means save persuasion; and similarly a state will not coerce or punish people for holding particular opinions, and a religion will not propagate its belief except by winning minds and consciences to accept it. The definition applies only if a man holds opinions. If a man holds no opinions or convictions, he is not being tolerant if he acquiesces in other people's; he is being indifferent. This needs to be emphasized. Indifference is not toleration; indifference is no virtue, the indifferent man exercises no self-restraint, no humility when he says he does not mind the opinions of others. To-day we need to be aware of the distinction. People steeped in the laziness of mental and moral indifference are apt to pride themselves on being so tolerant; they are not. Theirs is none of the nobility of those who with strong and passionate convictions yet discipline themselves painfully not to trample on the convictions of others, or those who perhaps with a hard struggle and occasional lapses combine zeal for a cause with courtesy towards its opponents. But to return. True tolerance implies convictions. The tolerant man, however, reverences the processes by which he reached his own convictions—the processes of reason, argument, intuition, conscience—and he therefore reverences the same processes at work in another man which lead that man to his own convictions. Here is the real test. If I am, *ex hypothesi*, a Roundhead it ought to give me no pleasure that Mr X is a Roundhead on the strength of ignorance, prejudice, or passion, and it ought to give me pleasure that Mr Y is a Cavalier if he is one out of reason and in an honest and good heart. That is why a party system, without actually violating toleration can, by partisan and emotional loyalties, undermine that reverence for personality which is the root of toleration.

So it seems that while the causes of toleration in history are complex and sometimes merely empirical—indeed Lord Balfour wrote that "toleration is one of the most valuable empirical maxims of modern politics"—as soon as we begin to explore its meaning we begin to dig down to something deeper than itself. Its deeper meaning is reverence for the other man because you believe something about him and about yourself. Aristotle describes the quality of ἐπιείκεια.

It is ἐπιείκεια [he wrote] to pardon human feelings and to look to the lawgiver not to the law, to the spirit not to the letter, to the intention not the action, to the whole and not to the part, to the character of the actor in the long run and not to the present moment, to remember good rather than evil, and good that one has received rather than good one has done, to bear being injured, to work to settle matters by words rather than deeds.[1]

St Paul used the same word "Let your ἐπιείκεια be known to all men":[2] A.V. translates 'moderation', R.V. translates 'forebearance', the *New English Bible* translates 'magnanimity'. The last seems nearer to the mind of one who also wrote this: "Charity suffereth long and is kind; charity envieth not; charity vaunteth not itself, doth not behave itself unseemly, is not easily provoked, thinketh no evil, rejoiceth not in iniquity but rejoiceth in the truth; beareth all things, believeth all things, hopeth all things, endureth all things."[3] St Paul's words are Greek, but the key word has a meaning deeply affected by the Jewish biblical history and the Jewish biblical conceptions. He was expressing the ethical corollaries of the Jewish and Christian faith that the worth of

[1] Aristotle, *Rhetoric*, 1.13.   [2] Phil. 4.5.   [3] 1 Cor. 13.4–7.

man is beyond utility, beyond time, nothing short of infinite, because of God's love for him, and because "the spirit of man is the candle of the Lord".[4]

Christians and Jews have not always been practisers of toleration. It is recorded that two of Christ's apostles wanted to ask for fire from heaven to destroy a Samaritan village which refused to receive their message, and Christ rebuked them. Too often Christians, and Churches, have followed the bad example of the two apostles and not the rebuke of Christ. Yet for all their failures and inconsistencies it is the truth about Man in the divine image, the truth which came from Palestine, which has so leavened the history of civilization that toleration has made its way forward. It rests upon divine sanctions, empiricism alone does not account for it.

To-day tolerance in the world is sorely tried. It is denied by Soviet Communism. Beyond the Iron Curtain the holding and propagation of opinions can be a crime and be punished as a crime. But how do we stand in the West? The older battles for tolerance are won. But new ones, more subtle and less generally perceived, need to be won. And they will be won only if the deepest meaning is given to tolerance, as virtues survive only if their implications move and grow. I think of two practical issues.

1. In a post-liberal civilization like ours, so different from a medieval one, one of the enemies to the virtue of toleration is not cruelty but indifferentism. Not caring, because nothing matters and nothing is true or false. This indifferentism assumes the cloak of toleration; but how intolerant it can become! It can be lazily intolerant of conviction, of principle, of dogma, of belief, of moral sanction. Do not let us in proclaiming the virtue of tolerance be afraid of having convictions, convictions which do not easily yield, which the lazy may call bigotry and narrowness. Christians and Jews are called by their own great traditions to the hard adventure of blending depth of conviction with the utmost reverence for the mind and conscience of other people, not for their flabbiness or laziness. A word here about the rôle of creeds and

[4] Prov. 20.27.

churches. Bishop Creighton used to say that we need to balance "the right of the individual to be free and the duty of the institution to be *something*". To be "something"; that seems modest enough. It is by their will to be "something" that churches serve tolerance and freedom.

2. On the other hand our western world is not yet free from the intolerance of race. Perhaps it is this which most of all calls us to go beyond tolerance and to see the insufficiency of tolerance as a conception. I need tolerance if I am to allow a man to have a different theology or different politics from my own. But if I am to allow a black man to live in my community it is not a matter of allowing his opinions but of allowing *him*; and while between my opinions and his opinions there can be an apathetic co-existence (which negatively is all that tolerance means), there cannot be merely that between one man and another man so long as the word *man* means what we believe it to mean. The alternative to racialism is not tolerance; it is those deeper virtues in our Jewish-Christian tradition into which tolerance must merge itself if the thing and the word are to survive.

Linked with tolerance in the tradition of the Waley Cohen Lecture is freedom. This has been often spoken about as if it were very simple, but it has more complexities even than tolerance. Tolerance begets tolerance in the cause of history. But one sort of freedom has been shown to destroy other kinds of freedom. Discussing freedom in the modern world in his book *Belief and Action*, Lord Samuel points out that the conflicts of the modern world have not been between power and freedom, but between one cause of freedom and another. It is interesting to recall some of the *naïveté* which the great theories of freedom involved. The Manchester school really believed that by creating freedom of trade between the nations you would cause all other kinds of freedom to follow inexorable progress, a theory which now seems so oddly parallel to the Marxist doctrine which grew partly in revolt from it. I quote Cobden, Manchester, 15 January 1846. "I believe", he says, "the physical gain will be the smallest gain to humanity from the success of this principle. I look farther; I see in the Free Trade principle that which shall act on the moral world as the principle of gravitation in the universe—drawing men together, thrusting aside the antagonism of race, and creed, and language, and uniting us in the bonds of eternal peace."

In the event it was in the midst of Cobdenite freedom that some of the worst frustrations of life for the working classes occurred. So too there was the confidence that freedom of suffrage and education would carry a host of other freedoms in its train. John Stuart Mill, whose own view came to be far more mature, thus describes the older view as his father, James Mill, had held it:

> The leading characteristics of the creed which we held in common with my father, may be stated as follows: an almost unbounded confidence in the efficacy of two things: representative government, and complete freedom of discussion. So complete was my father's reliance on the influence of reason over the minds of mankind, whenever it is allowed to reach them, that he felt as if all would be gained if the whole population were taught to read, if all sorts of opinions were allowed to be addressed to them by word and in writing, and if by means of the suffrage they could nominate a legislature to give effect to the opinions they adopted.[5]

The younger Mill was far more subtle, but, if he represented the old liberal doctrine in its most mature and its least naïve form, he prepared the way for its modification, and there came a new Liberalism which broke with *laissez-faire* and sought to protect and extend liberty by several forms of state intervention which would have made Cobden shudder. It is easy for us now to smile at the *naïveté* of the various phases of the modern cult of freedom. But we are not always ready to see and to state clearly the moral: that the root error was to regard man as competent in his own powers to forge progress for himself, and to forget that man is a creature and a sinner able to turn to corruption every advance that he makes. The maxim of Lord Acton that "power tends to corrupt and absolute power corrupts absolutely" may apply to

[5] J. S. Mill, *Autobiography*, World's Classics edn., p. 89.

the passions of democracies as well as to the cruelties of tyrants. Democracy is necessary to man's right fulfilment of himself, but it serves the true ends of its citizens only if it is animated by a sense of moral law and a sense of eternal worth of the individual man which reach far beyond itself.

What is man's true freedom? Just as the inadequacies of *tolerance* in history drive us to a deeper diagnosis of its meaning, so do the frustrations in the search for *freedom* drive us to a deeper diagnosis. We know that there is the freedom of a nation from foreign subjugation, the freedom of a people to make the laws they want, the freedom of an individual to think, believe, teach, and do what he pleases so long as he does not injure his fellows in ways which the State must prevent or punish. But in the pursuit of these freedoms one quest has again and again interfered with others, and new accessions of freedom create new frustrations. In depth, what is a man's freedom? Define it as his power to do just what he likes whenever he likes, and we find the definition breaking down. If I do just what I like on Monday, Tuesday, and Wednesday I may find that when Thursday comes there may be something I had ardently wanted to do, and I cannot get on with it because of the dissipations of the preceding days. The definition of my freedom as doing what I like whenever I like breaks down. Perhaps another definition will be more convincing: "to be able to choose a goal for myself and to unify my faculties in the consistent pursuit of that goal". If so, then my freedom involves for me some moral purpose, and discipline in its quest; and the nearer to perfection the purpose is the fuller will be my freedom. And the facts of experience as well as the breakdown of the secular quest of freedom in the modern world lead me to reaffirm that man's freedom is found in his obedience to God, "whom to serve is perfect freedom". Of old, St Augustine put this in the words *"cui servire regnare est"*. This is how a modern philosopher puts it, with greater sensitivity to modern minds. John Oman, after recalling that "dependence" is the characteristic attitude of religion, and "independence" the necessary condition of morality, says:

Only by being true to ourselves, can we find the reality which we must absolutely follow; yet, only by the sense of a reality we must absolutely follow, can we be true to ourselves. Thus our dependence and our independence would seem to be apart merely as strands of one cord, which have no strength except united.[6]

It follows that when we speak about "the free world" we must be sure what we mean. We rejoice in being free from the forms of mental and moral servitude which exist beyond the Iron Curtain. With those forms of servitude there can be no compromise. Yet we of the West need to be looking out for those dangers to our own freedoms which lurk within, for ways in which our freedom may be deepened, and we need above all to be looking to the foundation on which our freedom rests. I give some practical illustrations.

1. There is freedom of the mind. I wonder whether the sharp division which often exists in education between the arts mind and the science mind, or rather the technological mind, does not lead to a serious cramping of the mind. The over-specialization in so much education in the West can produce minds not trained to use the imagination and therefore stunted, however skilled they may be in certain fields. And does the rush, the noise, the busyness, the over-organization of our life give men and women the leisure and the power to reflect? If it fails to do so it prevents them from being their own true selves.

2. Economic freedom. Here the goal is still far away. One freedom stultifies another. It seems that in this country we may need new ways of economic planning in the interest of freedom. Left to themselves the present trends might create a London so overcrowded that its inhabitants are not free to move and a North of England whose sturdy people are not free to work.

3. The spreading of freedom. We cannot defend freedom in the West merely by building a rampart around it. We defend freedom by creating it and exporting it to those who lack it. The

[6] John Oman, *Grace and Personality*, p. 60.

countries which are prosperous must go to the aid of the countries where there is great poverty and hunger, and must give also of their spiritual resources wherever there is the will to receive them. There is still time to be given both to Africa and to Asia in helping their spiritual freedom and leadership for the future.

4. National sovereignty. The State has a divinely given rôle. But already in the past States have acknowledged obligations beyond themselves, as when they have bound themselves by covenant to take common actions for preserving the peace. How far may this now need to be carried? It is too big a question to discuss here and now. But let this be said. It will not infringe the true principle of freedom, rather will it accord with it, if ways of limiting the sovereignty of States are found.

So we of the West will be watchful about the subtle threats to our own freedom within, and for ways in which our freedom may grow. The freedom of nations, like the freedom of a man, lies in the discovery of divine purposes and in the reverent obedience to them. "It is not", said Burke, "what a lawyer tells me I may do, but what humanity, reason and justice tell me I ought to do." But all may be futile if we wander still further from the foundation, or fail to return to it while there is yet time. Our foundation is that religious God-fearing humanism which joined together the humanism of Greece and the God-fearing faith of Israel. There flowed into Europe from Palestine that ethical faith in One God which sees man not as autonomous and self-sufficient but as a creature and a sinner, exalted only when he humbles himself. That stream, flowing through the centuries, has often been hindered in its course by the follies of Christians and Jews, but flow it does. Just as it flowed into the ancient Graeco-Roman world and intermingled with Greek thought and Roman justice, so must it flow into our world of science so that religion and science to-day may intermingle, understand one another, and together help the world really to understand itself. For that stream gives meaning to freedom and to tolerance, and the world's predicament is that in place of the source of living water men hew them out cisterns, broken cisterns which hold no water.

Christian Spirituality
and the Modern World

I count it a privilege indeed to enjoy the hospitality of the Cercle
Oecumenique of the University of Louvain and to be allowed
to give this lecture within your walls to-day. For many years I
have revered the University of Louvain as a home of Catholic
learning, not least for its great contributions to studies, biblical,
patristic, and liturgical. These studies were never more important than they are to-day. I dare to take as my theme in this
lecture, "Christian spirituality and the modern world"; and it is
a theme which bears closely upon the Bible, the Fathers, and the
liturgy as well as upon many aspects of contemporary culture.
With a theme so wide you will expect me to do no more than
to draw together some simple and central principles. Nor will you
be surprised if I try to connect these principles with the great
cause of Christian unity.

THE NATURE OF
CHRISTIAN SPIRITUALITY

It is important to be sure of the distinctive meaning of Christian
spirituality amongst many other uses of the words "spiritual"
which are current. There is an idea of the "spiritual" as being
in total contrast with the "bodily" or the "material". That is not
the Christian conception. There is also an idea of the "spiritual"
as denoting particular aspects of man's character and achievement: his moral, aesthetic, and intellectual sensibilities in contrast with those elements in his being which are carnal or primitive. That likewise is not the Christian conception, for the higher
sensibilities in man can be corrupted no less than his carnal or

primitive instincts. No, Christian spirituality means the relation of a man or a woman to the Holy Spirit of God, the Spirit bestowed by Jesus Christ after his death, resurrection, and ascension. It is the mission of the Holy Spirit to indwell the Christian, influencing his entire life; and when a Christian is called a spiritual person it does not mean that his own spirit matters more than his body but that his whole being—body, soul, and spirit—is responding to the gracious rule of the Divine Spirit within.

Now if that be the essence of Christian spirituality it clearly has many facets. As the Spirit is the Spirit of truth, spirituality includes knowledge of the faith and of God who is the end of the faith. So too, because the Holy Spirit is the spirit of love, spirituality expresses itself in all the practical energies of Christian brotherhood and service. So too is spirituality inseparable from prayer and worship. It is the Spirit who enables the Christians to cry "Abba, Father", bearing witness with their spirits that they are sons of God.[1] The worship of Christians is always to be "in spirit and in truth".[2] It goes with a sacrificial self-consecration to God. The adjective "holy" itself speaks of that Godward consecration. Jesus consecrated himself in the offering on Calvary that the disciples might in turn be consecrated.[3] The Christians are a holy priesthood "to offer up spiritual sacrifices",[4] and they are enabled to do so inasmuch as Christ "through the eternal Spirit offered himself without spot to God".[5]

It is, however, possible to say that the last of those aspects of spirituality, namely worship, is primary and definitive, the key to the unity of all the aspects. Spirituality refers to a man's relation to God and it is the recovery in man of his basic and elementary relation to God the Creator. Man was created in God's own image, after God's own likeness in order to come to the perfection of fellowship with his Creator, a fellowship which the Biblical verb "to glorify" describes: a fellowship in which man reflects the character of his Creator so far as a creature can do so, humbling himself deeply before his Creator in utter dependence

---

[1] Rom. 8.15.   [2] John 4.23.   [3] John 17.17–19.
[4] 1 Pet. 2.5.   [5] Heb. 9.14.

and awaiting the open vision of him in heaven. That is the chief end of man. And when man, redeemed by Christ, is given the Holy Spirit to rule his life he is enabled to recapture the elemental relation of child and creature. The Holy Spirit is the Spirit of our present sonship, and he is no less the Spirit who anticipates within us the glory of heaven. That is why St Peter calls him "the spirit of glory",[6] and the author of the Epistle to the Hebrews calls him "the powers of the world to come".[7]

To say all this is to say that the worship of God is itself the inner core of Christian spirituality; the heart, the mind, and the will directed towards the glory of God as man's goal. Every time that a Christian lifts up his soul to God in desire towards him he is, however faintly, realizing that fellowship with the Creator for which he was created, and he is, in a tiny and yet significant way, anticipating the goal of heaven. Thus regarded, spirituality is no escape from the world. It is lived out in all the complexities of our social life, in family, city, country, industry, culture, joy, and sorrow; for it is the spirituality of a man, and a man is involved in all these things. It is inseparable from service, love, duty, the moulding of the common life. Yet in deep-down essence it is the spirit of worship. Allow me to quote some words of a former Archbishop of Canterbury, William Temple. He said: "It is sometimes supposed that conduct is primary, and worship helps it. That is incorrect. The truth is that worship is primary, and conduct tests it." How many of your great Catholic teachers have taught the same!

THE DISRUPTION OF SPIRITUALITY IN THE MODERN WORLD

Now I pass on to consider with you the disruption of spirituality in the modern world. I will not speak of Asia or Africa, where the problems are different, although those lands are of great importance for us all. I speak of the West, of Europe, of England, and of America. Here we are the heirs of centuries of civilization;

[6] 1 Pet. 4.14.   [7] Heb. 6.5.

22

and while civilization may be long and deeply penetrated by the influence of Christianity, it is impossible that civilization and Christianity can be precisely equated. To-day we see many features in civilization to be far removed from the obedience of Christ. I attempt no deep diagnosis if I mention some features of civilization which militate against the spirituality about which we are thinking.

There is the widespread idea that man is competent by his own powers to organize his own progress and happiness. It is a strange idea, inasmuch as the world is deeply divided and unable to rid itself of terrible weapons of destruction. Yet the idea is there because man does not sit back and ask himself the question "quo tendimus?" so much as press on absorbed in the use of his powers and the fascination of them. The mind which enjoys its own creations in discovery, in technology, in the organization of human welfare, can become too busy and absorbed to question man's own competence. Hence in the midst of man's mature intellectuality there is the pride and the insensitivity to the Spirit of God which creates what we call "modern secularism".

Then there is the tendency for modern man to live in a whirl with his mind overcrowded. There are so many more things nowadays to think about, and so many impressions entering the mind in rapid succession, while there are still only sixty minutes in each hour and only twenty-four hours in each day. Hence the mind of man tends to lose its freedom and to be ruled by the flux of impressions and sensations. I sometimes think that in the circumstances of the modern world an important part of our Christian asceticism needs to be the discipline of the mind to secure its freedom even more than the discipline of the body.

There is, as a result of the loss of touch with God, a deep frustration and fear, often subconscious and always divisive in its effects upon man's soul. Is not the considerable over-emphasis upon sex in some of our population due less to any increase in the power of sexual impulses than to an urge to escape frustration by the sense of achievement which sexual adventure can provide? I agree with those who say that frankness and openness about sex is highly to be desired, as sex is one of the Creator's good gifts. But the obsession with sex denotes in part a flight from frustration and in part a severance of the bond which unites sex and the other elements in personality which all together find fulfilment in marriage and the family.

It is when the Creator is forgotten that his gifts and creatures are allowed to dominate and to become ends in themselves. So it is that technology, or money, or comfort, or sex can rule man, instead of having their true place, which is to be ruled by man for the glory of God. So we have a society where man, mature in his powers of mind and spirit, loses his freedom and loses his way to God.

THE MISSION OF SPIRITUALITY: INVOLVEMENT

In the world as we know it how must Christian spirituality express itself? There are still the two aspects of the Christian way, inseparable in essence but describable only in duality.

There is the rôle of detachment in the adoration of God. There is the rôle of involvement in the service of the world.

The second of these, the involvement, is very prominent in contemporary Christian thinking as the use of such terms as "apostolate" and "the apostolate of the laity" shows. These terms describe the Christian mission to go where the people are, and to bring to them, not as it were from above but from along-side, the treasures of Christian faith. I know that in Belgium, as in France and in England and in many countries there is a new endeavour to bring the Christian faith to the workers in the big factories and industrial units.

The involvement of Christians in the service of the world has, however, many aspects. There is their service in the cause of peace. There is their service in the cause of the hungry and the homeless, where the need is for countries which are prosperous to bring to the countries where there is hunger the resources and the technical skill to enable them to grow more food for their people. Here are illustrations of Christian actions which are an inseparable part of Christian spirituality. I recall the prophetic words of St Chrysostom that it is vain to come to the altar in the Eucharist unless we go out to find the altar which is identical with the poor brother. "This altar thou mayest see everywhere lying in lanes and in market places, and thou mayest sacrifice upon it every hour. When thou seest a poor brother, reflect that thou beholdest an altar."[8] These are no more than illustrations of that service of humanity which is a part of Christian spirituality.

Meanwhile the secular world, estranged from God as it is, is not without its gropings after God. These gropings express themselves sometimes in a kind of secular spirituality, a feeling after moral values and ultimate meaning though the Christian dogma is rejected and the name of God be discarded. To this secular spirituality Christian people have a duty and a message.

In this connection there are some Protestant theologians who have encouraged the idea of a "Christianity without religion"; "Let us", they say in effect, "try to find God and to present God not within the realm of religious practice but within the moral perceptions of secular man, and within the meeting of persons with persons." There was Dietrich Bonhoeffer, the Lutheran pastor who suffered in a concentration camp and before his death in 1945 put forward in his *Letters from Prison* the idea that religion was outmoded and that Christianity without religion will hold the future. So too a Protestant theologian still living, Paul Tillich, has tried to show how secular man may find God not by looking to the language of the Church but looking deep down within the meaning of his own existence: "he who knows about depth, knows about God". These thoughts, for all the novelty of their expression, are not far from thoughts to be found in some of the Catholic mystical writers of the past. It is possible, therefore, to make a positive approach towards them. When secular man finds in the depths of his being reality, ultimate, imperative, personal, we can say to him as St Paul said to the Athenians, "whom ye worship in ignorance, him declare we unto you".

[8] Homily XX, on 1 Corinthians.

25

Yet the concept of "Christianity without religion" calls for critical scrutiny. "Religion" can mean our own pious self-consciousness and the devout atmosphere of words and thoughts which go therewith. Well is it that men should look for God not there but in the midst of the world's agony. "Religion" in this sense was described by the Catholic theologian Père de Lubac thus: "the selfish piety, the narrow religious outlook, the neglect of ordinary duties in the multiplication of 'devotions', the swamping of the devotional 'life' by the detestable 'I', the failure to realize that prayer is essentially the prayer of all for all".[9] If we have that kind of picture of religion, whether amongst Catholics or amongst Protestants, we can understand the desire to have Christianity without it. But, when all the accretions of pietism have been pruned away, religion remains as a native and elemental impulse of man, rooted in his relation as creature to God as Creator. Religion is the longing, often smothered and distorted, in the words, *Fecisti nos ad te, Domine, et cor nostrum inquietum est donec requiescat in te.*

THE MISSION OF SPIRITUALITY: DETACHMENT

It is clear, however, that with the involvement of service to the world there is united, in true Christian spirituality, a spirit of detachment. While Christian people strive to heal the world's ills by their service and charity, it is for them also to point to the ill which is at the root of all ills, the estrangement of the world from God, and to witness to the reality of God himself. They do so by the depth of their communion with him and by their humility before him. The unknown writer of the Epistle to Diognetus said, "As the soul is in the body so are the Christians in the world". The Christians serve a world which has lost its soul by the lifting up of their own souls in adoration.

Adoration and communion with God is, however, always the soul's response to God's own gift. This divine gift is seen in the

[9] *Catholicism*, p. x.

Bible as the Word of God. The Word of God is both speech and action. By the Word of God the people of Israel were delivered from bondage in Egypt and made the recipients of the divine covenant and the divine law at Sinai. So too by the Word of God the people of the new Israel were delivered from sin and death and given the new covenant in the blood of Jesus the Messiah. The action of the Divine Word, both in the Old Testament and in the New, creates and sustains a people, the Church, the family of the redeemed; and it is within this corporate life that the divine gifts are brought to individual souls. The sacred Scriptures tell of the divine history and the divine gifts, and in the *Lectio Divina* the members of the Church refresh their souls with the knowledge of them and are drawn to the response of thanksgiving and adoration. But there is more. The Word of God was made flesh in the birth of Jesus, and came to indwell the Church through the sacraments, and the action of the Holy Spirit. The divine gift is thus not only the record of God's gracious acts long ago in the days of the Bible. It is also the very presence of Jesus, God and Man, here and now—contemporary: Jesus who is *Verbum caro factum* and is no less *Christus crucifixus resurrectus et glorificatus*. The mystery of the Church is *Christus in vobis, spes gloriae*.

In the worship of the Church there are three chief elements: the eucharistic liturgy, the divine office, and personal prayer both vocal and mental. The last may happen in groups and families as well as individually. I use the terms—liturgy, divine office, personal prayer—familiar to you and familiar also to me as an Anglican. In each of the three elements, eucharist, office, personal prayer there is the divine gift and the human response.

The Eucharist is the centre and norm of all worship. There the Divine Word is revealed in the lections and propers for the nourishment of our souls. But at the climax of the rite, through the consecration prayer, the whole mystery of Christ as priest, victim, and victor, is present. In the eucharistic canon gift and response find fullness of expression, and both are inseparable from Christ himself. The divine gift to us is Christ, and so too the response from man is Christ, himself our sacrifice. Our own response is made only as we are ourselves "in Christ". In the words of an Anglican eucharistic hymn, we say:

> Look, Father, look on his anointed face,
> And only look on us as found in him.

But let me quote also the words of St Augustine: "This is the sacrifice of Christians, the many one body in Christ, which also the Church celebrates in the sacrament of the altar, familiar to the faithful, where it is shown to be that in this thing which she offers she herself is offered."[1]

I speak of liturgy as a fact in Christendom which has appeared in a variety of forms and phases, with different spiritual emphasis. In the Latin rite there is a vivid sense of the Cross where sinful men and women look upon him whom their sins have pierced and know that in Jesus crucified alone is salvation, though the thought of the heavenly tabernacle is never far away. In the liturgies of the Orthodox East, both Greek and Slavonic, the joy of the Resurrection is prominent and the worshippers know themselves to be already in the heavenly places in Christ. In the case of Anglican liturgy it is necessary for a right understanding to see not only the rite in England, but also the rites in the United States (derived from Scotland), in Canada, in the West Indies, in India, and in various parts of Africa, giving as they do a picture of a growing liturgical life mindful alike of the one sacrifice of Calvary and of the heavenly priesthood of our Lord. To-day liturgical movements in many parts of Christendom put a renewed emphasis upon the participation of the faithful in the liturgy and upon the down-to-earth aspect of the liturgy as the means of consecrating the common, everyday life of the people to God. In this way liturgy is seen to belong alike to the involvement and to the detachment in the mission of the Church.

While, however, the liturgy is the norm of worship, there is the need for the divine gift so to penetrate the souls of Christian people that they are drawn into the deep response of penitence,

[1] *De Civitate Dei* x.6.

love, and adoration, through meditative and contemplative prayer. Without meditative and contemplative prayer the sacramental life can become shallow and formal and can lack interior depth. It is essential that the liturgical movement with its great emphasis upon the corporate action of the faithful in worship be accompanied by no less emphasis upon interior prayer.

It would be rash of me to venture far into the controversial subject of the relation between meditation and contemplation, and between activity and passivity in prayer. But these matters are fundamental. In modern times in our Anglican Church as well as in Catholic spirituality in Europe there came about a tendency to regard discursive meditation (called by whatever name) as a norm for most Christians and to think of any approach to contemplative prayer as a thing far removed and characteristic of advanced souls or mystics. But we have seen the recovery of an older tradition of spirituality, whereby elementary contemplation has a place not only for advanced souls but for ordinary Christians too. This older tradition is beautifully described by Dom Cuthbert Butler, a former Abbot of the Benedictine Monastery of Downside, in his book *Western Mysticism*. I would myself humbly dare to say that whereas discursive meditation can become all too easily a cerebral process, putting too much strain upon the powers of the mind, affective prayer or elementary contemplation is God's gift to many who are ready to reach out to God in desire and longing. This contemplative prayer is something which God can grant to souls who reach out to him in their poverty, their want, their childlike desire. It is a prayer which some writers describe as coming "from the ground of the soul". I believe that the capacity of the ordinary Christian for contemplation is greater by far than some of our theories of the spiritual life have allowed.

It is in the measure in which the contemplative spirit is present in the Church that the reality of God will be grasped within the Church's multiple activities. "Contemplare et contemplata aliis tradere" was a maxim of St Dominic. But the practice of this maxim demands a will for leisure and passivity in the midst of ceaseless activity—a will *vacare considerationi*. I recall the words of Fénelon in a letter to a French duke of the time, "I want to help you to find how to lead a very full and yet a leisurely life". That is a prime requisite for Christian spirituality in the modern world.

THROUGH SPIRITUALITY
TO UNITY

I come finally to the relation betwen spirituality and unity. Many hearts in every part of Christendom have been warmed by the actions and words of Pope John in showing his own deep longing *ut unum sint*. The obstacles are many and obvious, and among them are the differences of dogma. It is only "speaking truth in love" to acknowledge these; it is unreal to minimize them.

It is, however, on the plane of spirituality that we can with great profit search for unity, less in the thoughts and formulations of the mind than in the depths of the soul and those actions which are controlled from thence. I think of Roman Catholics praying perhaps in the manner taught by St Sulpice, "Christ before the eyes, Christ in the heart, Christ in the hands". I think of Eastern Orthodox Christians praying perhaps the prayer which came from Mount Sinai called "The Jesus Prayer", drinking the name of Jesus into the soul along with the rhythms of human breath. I think of Anglican Christians coming to the liturgy, now celebrated daily in many of our cathedrals and parish churches, and commemorating the sacrifice of Calvary and feeding upon the Body and Blood of the Lord together with the divine Word in the scriptures. Here indeed is a unity found in the depths of the soul. But it is more. It includes the use of the sacred scriptures as *divina lectio*, and at least the concept of liturgy as *mysterium Christi*; furthermore the unity in the depths of the soul is possible only because of the Holy Spirit by whom alone Christians can pray "Abba Father". It is a baptismal unity, a unity—however unconsummated, however incomplete—which is real in virtue of the fact of Holy Baptism.

This unity in the depths of spirituality is something which I would not exaggerate alongside the requirements of the whole unity in dogma and life. Yet I could not belittle this unity of spirituality, for it has its own theological implications in terms of Holy Baptism, as well as its practical implications in terms of the united witness of those who are baptized. But rather than try to develop these theological implications—for we still see through a glass darkly—I would end within the limits of my chosen theme: Christian spirituality and the modern world. Wherever there is Christian spirituality there is already a link between souls on earth and the very life of heaven, and there is already a recovery of the inner soul of Christendom. Already, even in a tiny way, there is fulfilment of the old Gelasian prayer "that things which were cast down may be raised up, that things which had grown old may be made new and that all things may return unto unity through him by whom all things were made".

Heaven and Hell

When I was honoured by the invitation to visit New College and to give the Drew Lecture to-day my mind turned quickly to the names of some of the great teachers of theology who belonged to the College in the past. To one of these my own debt is immense—Peter Taylor Forsyth. It is hard to think of a theologian who exhibited so thoroughly as he the central place of the Cross in Christianity. He was concerned as a teacher with many of the great Christian doctrines, but he saw all of them in the light of that relation of sinful man and holy God which the Cross discloses. To him heaven was the adoration of the Lamb as it had been slain.

When once I had chosen Heaven and Hell as my subject for to-night I turned for help to the writings of Forsyth. And not in vain, for I lighted upon this arresting passage:

> Prayer is the nature of our hell as well as our heaven. Our hell is ceaseless, fruitless, hopeless gnawing prayer, prayer which cannot stop, prayer which is addressed to nothing, and obtaining nothing. And prayer is our heaven. It goes home to God, and attains there and rests there.[1]

These words are puzzling, and it is *after* we have wrestled with our subject that their meaning may come home to us. So I will return to them later. Yet at once the words convey this to us, that heaven and hell, far off though they be, are related closely to the here and now, giving intensity to the present moment.

It would be easy in speaking about heaven and hell to wander into doctrines which stand near to them in the Christian scheme, such as the doctrine of the Communion of Saints with its bond of the living and the departed in mutual prayer and praise, or the

[1] *The Soul of Prayer*, new edition, p. 61.

32

doctrine of the state of those who have died in faith. Let me mention in this connection only that it seems clear that, when our Lord told the dying thief that he would be with him that day in Paradise and when St Paul spoke of death as to depart and to be with Christ, the implication is plain that the departed are in a state of consciousness and of personal relationship in fellowship with Christ; but it is not to be assumed that perfection or final glory is at once bestowed after death.

But my present task is to consider with you not this intermediate state of grace and patience, pain and joy, but the finalities, Heaven and Hell. Yet one preliminary theme must needs prepare our way. It is resurrection. The sequence of the Creed reminds us that we should think first about the resurrection of the dead before we think about the life of the world to come. It is upon the Resurrection that the Christian hope is based, and resurrection belongs both to our present state as Christians and to the final destiny.

First, then, resurrection is a mighty act of God. Remember that in the New Testament the language used is not of Jesus rising but of Jesus being raised by God. Jesus did not "achieve" resurrection. Rather did he make himself nought, and when all was dark, when human possibilities were exhausted, God raised him by a mighty act of his power. This truth about resurrection colours the whole process of man's movements towards his goal, whether in this world or the next. It is not that man, even under God's grace, gets gradually better and better and so attains to saintliness here and to heaven thereafter. Rather does the grace of God work surprises, turning defeats into deliverances, "calling things that are nought as though they are", and acting beyond any laws of progress or expectation. We have no rights here, and no rights hereafter. Unprofitable servants at every stage, we know that the Christian life has always the two facets: on the one side there is the God who raises the dead and on the other side there is "faith alone".

Secondly, the resurrection of Jesus is the prelude to the resurrection of those who believe in him and are united to him by

faith and baptism. I need not recall to you the many references
to this in the New Testament.[2] Already the Christians united
with Christ are raised together with him. Already they are par-
takers of Christ, possessors of his life-giving Spirit, sharers in
eternal life; St Paul and St John are at one in affirming this
present realization. But there is a "not yet", and a consummation
still to come. Though they are already "in Christ" the Christians
are still living in this world, they belong to cities, states, and
nations. They are involved in suffering, and in sin which con-
tradicts their Christian status. But amid this ambiguous interim
they await a future glory. It will be an unveiling in perfection of
a union with Christ at present hidden and incomplete. It will be
"the coming of Christ", "the resurrection", "the glory". It must
be wrong to try to be literalistic about the imagery used to express
the inexpressible, for "eye hath not seen, nor ear heard, neither
have entered into the heart of man, the things which God hath
prepared for them that love him".[3]

Thus through the doctrine of resurrection in the New Testament, with its double strain of something already realized and
something "not yet", we approach the doctrine of heaven. Here
let the word "glory" guide us in our approach. It is one of the
marvellous words of the Bible, for it tells of heaven and the last
things and it also tells of man and the first things. So it is; God
created man in his own image in order that he might come to
perfect fellowship with his Creator. It is a fellowship of intimacy,
love, and knowledge intermingled with awe and dependence as,
for all the intimacy, the line between Creator and creature ever
remains. It is this blending of intimacy and dread dependence, of
man reflecting the Creator's character and humbly ascribing all to
him, which the Bible describes by the words *glory* and *glorify*.
There is the secret of man's existence and of his rôle in the created
world, and the clue to man's destiny. Heaven is the final consummation of this, for heaven is man finding himself in the glory
of his Maker.

[2] Cf. Rom. 6.1–11; Col. 3.1–4.   [3] 1 Cor. 2.9.

So we approach the thought of heaven. Let me now quote St Augustine, in words rooted in the Bible: "We shall rest, and we shall see: we shall see, and we shall love; we shall love, and we shall praise. Behold, what shall be in the end, which is no end."[4]

There is "a description of heaven". Let us follow the description through.

"We shall rest." There is in modern religion a strain of discontent with the idea of heaven as rest. Why, we are told, should repose and inactivity be the goal of energetic men and women? Hence the modern reaction from the phrase "rest in peace" upon tombstones, and the liking for words like "called to higher service". But these modern ideas are not profound, and they belong to a secularized view of religion. How profound in contrast is St Augustine's word *vacabimus*: we shall have a vacation. We shall cease from our restless busyness, from doing things for the sake of doing them; and, purged of the egotisms of our own activity, we shall for once be passive and in our passivity realize that it is God who works. So in this passivity our eyes will be open, and we shall see. *Videbimus*, we shall be freed so as to see God in his perfect beauty, and "blessed are the pure in heart, for they shall see God". It will be a vision glorious and satisfying, the goal for which we were created. And as we see God in his beauty we shall begin to reflect him, for the seeing will be in a purity of love whereby his love becomes our own. This reflection of him will mean that we love, love him and all his creatures. *Amabimus*, we shall love our fellows and be serving them selflessly; the second great commandment will be perfectly fulfilled in the realization of the first. Serving our neighbours we shall rejoice in them and with them; and we shall as never before enjoy our fellow creatures. But in the midst of this love, service, enjoyment we shall be aware as never before that God is the giver and God is the goal; and in full circle the heart which has moved from God to creatures will be drawn back to God in praise and wonder. *Laudabimus*, we shall praise God, rejoicing to give to him all that

[4] *De Civitate Dei* xxii 30

35

is his due. If the Latin verbs in St Augustine's description have till now served as well as words can serve, here the Latin *laudare* scarcely matches the Greek δοξάζειν, the giving glory to God which is the crown of heaven's meaning. Rest, see, love, praise— each leads on to the other, and all interpenetrate *in fine sed non in fine*, in the end which is no end.

Such will be a perfection in which the contradictions familiar in our present existence are resolved. At present we oscillate between *possession* and *discovery*. We know at times the happiness of arrival and achievement. But this can soon be dulled, and we set out again to find the happiness of the chase, of search, struggle, and exploration. In heaven, however, the joy of arrival and possession and the joy of exploration are one; for while all is perfect there is within perfection a ceaseless discovery of novelty— it is ever a new song that is sung before the throne. So too we experience here the contrast between *rest* and *action*; rest is enjoyable but it can become boring, and so we plunge into activity, but activity after satisfying us awhile can tire us and make us long for rest. In heaven, rest and action are one; the saints rest from their labours, and their works follow them. Our peace is in the will of God, *semper agens, semper quietus*. So too in our present experience we never escape the antinomy between *worship* and *service*. We speak often of their unity, but we know in practice the tension between them. In heaven worship and service are utterly one. There is "no temple there", for all is worship, and "his servants shall serve him, and they shall see his face". Thus will our familiar contradictions disappear in the glory of God.

As heaven is that glory, there can be no idea of it as a selfish compensation for life's frustrations, or as "pie in the sky when you die". No selfish desires can lead a man towards heaven as heaven is the very contradiction of selfishness. There is indeed a doctrine of reward in the teaching of Christ. But the good works which win reward are the outcome of God's reign in God-centred lives, and can never be a selfish investment. And the reward to which good works prepare the way cannot be quantitative as it is the reward of being with God in his presence.

The hope of heaven is one aspect of the Christian hope which the New Testament formulates in more ways than one. Besides the hope of heaven there is the hope of the coming of the reign of God in history. The Christians pray "thy kingdom come on earth as it is in heaven". Since love is one and indivisible there is no separation between the love wherewith we serve humanity in Christ's name and bear witness to his reign on earth, and the love which is eternal life and the anticipation of heaven itself. Thus we cannot pursue the quest of heaven without a concern about God's reign in history, and equally our concept of God's reign in history will be secularized and robbed of depth if we are negligent of the hope of heaven and our present heavenly citizenship.

Just as we cannot conceive the reign of God in history apart from heaven which is beyond history, so too we are encouraged by scripture and the Christian tradition to think of things terrestrial as not abolished but fulfilled in heaven. That is the significance of the Resurrection of the Body. It does not necessarily mean the "resurrectio huius carnis" understood by some of the Latin Fathers; rather does it mean that there will be in heaven fullness of personal expression, of recognition, and of the characteristics through which people have been known and loved in this present life. "Non eripit mortalia, qui regna dat caelestia." The doctrine of the *final* resurrection of bodies to complete the beatitude of the saints conveys in symbol the truth that the perfection of the one is inseparable from the perfection of all those who are to be made perfect. The joy of one is incomplete without the joy of all.

Will, however, some be lost? The teaching of Christ in the Gospel of St Matthew ends with a pair of parables of judgement, describing the fate of those within and those without the covenant. The first is the parable of the talents. It tells of how those who have received gifts will be judged in accordance with their use of them. The second is the parable of the sheep and the goats. It tells of how all the nations, the Gentiles outside the covenant, are gathered at a final assize; and they are judged by their response to the natural law of kindness and charity—a response by which, all unknowing, they have been either ministering to Christ or spurning him. "Inasmuch as ye did it unto these my brethren, ye did it unto me." We learn from this that those who have had no chance of being confronted with the knowledge and truth of Christ are judged in accord with the light which conscience has given them.

But both of these parables of judgement end with a description of loss, the one describing it as "outer darkness" and the other as "the fire of the age to come". Is there a hell? Can a man, be he a believer or be he an unbeliever, exclude himself from heaven?

The *credibility* of hell rests upon the concept of human freedom. Our freedom is the condition of our human dignity, of our being creatures who are not automata but can will to love or not to love, of our place in a world based upon love and not upon mechanism, of our adherence to an ethical theism. I am free. Rob me of my power to separate myself from the love of God and to shut myself in darkness, and you rob me of the freedom whereby I know myself the child and creature of the holy Father. This exclusion is hell, the self-exclusion of those who prefer to be isolated in self-love because they want it so to be. Theoretically it is hard to see how the loss can be *eternal*, for, as F. D. Maurice insisted, eternity is the quality of God and of the life shared with him. Theoretically, it could be everlasting. But is it? We have to ask what has been *revealed* by Christ.

Christ describes the loss and punishment of those excluded from him at the judgement, and the adjective in the Gospels is αἰώνιος which some would translate "everlasting" and others "of the aeon to come". We are reckoning with imagery, and imagery is poetical. We need not be compelled to take literally the fire and the gnawing worm, nor perhaps the language of duration. We know that there was a tendency in the early Church to elaborate the imagery of apocalyptic in the tradition of the word of Jesus, as a comparison of some parallel passages in St Mark and St Matthew shows.[5] Yet when full allowance has been made for sayings which are poetic rather than literal and for the possibility

[5] Cf., e.g. Mark 13.23-7 and Matt. 24.25-31; Mark 10.29 and Matt. 19.28.

of elaborations in the gospel tradition, it is impossible to eliminate sayings of Jesus which give terrible warning as to the possibility of loss and exclusion.[6] Warnings against loss of salvation are there, incisive and inexorable. What the state of loss may be like or how many may be lost, we do not know. It is one of those matters where our Lord seems to give us not definitions, nor answers to our curiosity, but warning and challenge. "Are there few that be saved?" asks Peter, and our Lord answers "strive to enter by the strait gate".[7] We put the warning to ourselves, and we make our own the words:

> King of Majesty tremendous,
> Who dost free salvation send us,
> Fount of pity, thou defend us.
> Think, kind Jesus, my salvation
> Caused thy wondrous Incarnation,
> Leave me not to reprobation.

Heaven and hell are called the last things. But they are anticipated daily in the here and now. Every act of faith and charity, every movement of heart and mind towards God are anticipations of heaven. The Christian Eucharist is a little sharing in heaven's worship, and the Holy Spirit working in us is the first fruits of the heavenly inheritance, the power already of the age to come. So too is hell anticipated whenever men isolate themselves in pride and selfishness and make barriers between one another and their Creator. Our life as Christians is one of conflict and ambiguity; we live under grace and yet sin dies very hard within us. Thus heaven and hell already do battle, and the conflict between them may be raging within our prayers as well as our actions. So I return to the words of P. T. Forsyth with which I started.

Prayer is the nature of our hell as well as our heaven. Our hell is ceaseless, fruitless, hopeless gnawing prayer, prayer which cannot stop, prayer which is addressed to nothing and obtaining

6 See Mark 14.21; Matt. 7.22–3; Luke 13.26–8; Matt. 10.28; Luke 12.5; 13.23–4.
7 Luke 13.24.

nothing. And prayer is our heaven. It goes home to God and attains there and rests there.

Now prayer is characteristic of piety, and it is plain enough that to be pious is not necessarily to be near to heaven. As with works, so with piety. There can be good works done with zeal and energy, and yet there can be in them a self-conscious busyness or a possessiveness and patronage which leaves the doer in the bondage of self and far indeed from heaven. There can be piety which dwells upon the man's own spiritual state and his self-conscious enjoyment of it, a piety concerned with its own exterior techniques or its own interior feelings, and the devout man can be far indeed from heaven. Philanthropy and piety alike may be nearer to hell than to heaven. But wherever there are works in which God is present through the humility and charity of the doer heaven is not far off. And wherever there is the prayer of a soul hungry for God and ready amidst its own weakness and failure to be filled with God's own charity, the *vacare* being the gate to the *amare*, heaven is very near. So, not only amid the conflicts of the world but within the soul of the Christian as he prays, heaven and hell struggle together like the twins in the womb of Rebekah, and both are near to us at every moment.

Christianity and the Supernatural

Amid all the points of contrast between the Bible and the outlook of the modern world none is perhaps greater than that which is provided by the miraculous element in the Biblical narratives. In this lecture on the Ethel M. Wood foundation which it is my great privilege to be giving in the University I do no more than try to clarify some of the questions which arise concerning the miracles in the Gospels in relation to divine revelation. If I set the questions in a wide context it is because I think that only in that wide context are the questions intelligible at all.

I

Ninety-eight years ago James B. Mozley, the Regius Professor of Divinity in the University of Oxford, gave a series of Bampton lectures with the title *On Miracles*. It was his thesis that miracles are the necessary guarantee of divine revelation. Since revelation means a communication from God to man it is important to be certain that statements which claim to be revelation, as for instance the teachings of Christ and the apostles, are without doubt given from God. The necessary proof of this is available when the teaching is accompanied by miracles; it is these which guarantee the claim of the words to be revelation. Thus, while revelation is in its content beyond reason, the presence of miracle alone makes our acceptance of it rational. The Mohammedan is irrational in that he accepts the Prophet's assertions unattested; indeed Mozley goes so far as to say that because of the absence of miracles in his religious scheme the Mohammedan "shows an utterly barbarous idea of evidence and a total miscalculation of the claims of reason which unfits his religion for an enlightened age and people".[1]

To-day exceedingly few, if any, exponents either of the concept of revelation or of the Gospels would put the matter in that way. Indeed in 1865 this view of miracle was already becoming obsolescent, and its publication by J. B. Mozley seems now to have been rather a rearguard action on behalf of a view more characteristic of the eighteenth century, wherein both the great Bishop Butler and the well-known Archdeacon Paley had successively held it. If to-day a different view of miracle dominates the theological scene it is partly because a more scientific study of the Gospels shows that the Gospels themselves do not present the miracles in purely evidential terms, and partly because the supernatural is understood in a way significantly different from the way in which Mozley understood it.

What do we understand by the supernatural? "Well," said Humpty Dumpty, "when I use a word it means just what I choose it to mean." And anyhow *some* word is required to express the phenomena inherent in the divine activity in the world, if there is a living God who has a dynamic relation to the world and to human beings, and if providence, grace, and revelation have any place at all. Divine grace is the most intelligible illustration. If God acts upon human beings so as to have moral and spiritual, and perhaps physical, effects upon them, if divine grace can create saintly lives, if sacraments are divine operations for the believer's good, then the word supernatural serves to express this. Within the wide phenomenon of the supernatural, and just how wide it would be hard to dogmatize, the miraculous as Christian tradition knows it is but one element. The supernatural need not in its actions override the known laws of nature, but when it does so the further, specific term "miracle" becomes appropriate. It is not the only mode of the supernatural, and the supernatural includes not only events like the raising of Lazarus from death but also events like the turning of Saul the Pharisee into Paul the

[1] J. B. Mozley, *On Miracles*, p. 31.

Christian or like the sacraments wherein divine grace does not annul nature so much as use nature for moral ends.

There is therefore a big difference between the view of miracle which isolates it as Butler, Paley, and Mozley did, and the view which sees it in a context of the supernatural more widely understood. That the former view yielded place within the nineteenth century was due, I think, not only to trends in philosophy and Biblical study but also to religious movements. Religious movements as different as the revivalism of John Wesley, the romanticism of Coleridge, and the sacramentalism of the Tractarians had a share in setting miracle in the wider context, for all these religious teachers were conscious of analogies between miracle and the work of grace in human lives. To John Wesley the works of Christ were continued in the greater works done by the disciples; and Wesley says, "the change wrought by the Holy Spirit in the heart is equivalent to all outward miracles, as implying the self-same power which gave sight to the blind, feet to the lame, and life to the dead".[2] As to evidences, this experiential approach sees the supernatural as significantly in divine grace in the soul as in external miracles, and belief in revelation owes as much to the one kind of evidence as to the other.

Let it, however, be said that this latter conception, new as it was to a certain scholastic tradition, was far from new in the history of Christendom. The ancient Fathers had delighted to trace the analogies of miracle in the souls of Christians. St Augustine saw miracle not only there, but in nature too. "Though these miracles of nature be no longer admired, yet ponder them wisely, and they are more astonishing than the strangest; for man himself is a greater miracle than all he can work."[3] And when we go back to the New Testament we find the same conception. The Holy Spirit, who is himself the essence of the supernatural in the experience of the apostolic Church, is made known miraculously in the rushing wind, the fiery tongues, the speaking with tongues on the day of Pentecost; but no less significantly when St Paul says that "the fruit of the Spirit is love, joy, peace, longsuffering,

[2] Wesley, *Sermons*, 1825 edition, i. 234.   [3] *De Civitate Dei* x. 12.

gentleness, goodness, faith, meekness, temperance";[4] and whereas he claims himself to be highly competent in one of the supernatural gifts called "speaking with tongues", he names love to be the greatest of them all.[5]

So too in the Gospels the miracles are seen not as an isolated intrusion of divine power, but against a wide and continuous background of divine power—of the supernatural. To Jesus, God is everywhere at work. Nature is the perpetual scene of the providential actions of his intimate fatherly care, and the disciples are bidden to have their eyes open to God's graciousness and God's demands thereby conveyed. No less vividly is God at work in history, especially in the history and the scriptures of the chosen people. So too it is of God's power that proud men can become like little children, that Simon Peter is given a gift of faith coming not from flesh and blood but from the Father in heaven, that everything will be given to the man who prays in faith. Indeed it is doubtful whether the man who is blind to the divine working in familiar things will benefit from the most startling miracle. "If they hear not Moses and the prophets, neither will they be persuaded though one rose from the dead." [6]

II

So we turn now to examine the Gospels again, to see how the evangelists present the miracles and what meaning they assign to them and believe that Jesus assigned to them.

1. The Synoptists first. The miracles wrought by Jesus are called not "wonders" but "works". Specifically they are works of the kingdom, or reign of God.

Jesus preaches in Galilee that the reign of God is imminent, indeed present already. The reign is set forth in the righteousness which Jesus teaches, and the childlike and the penitent can receive it. The reign is also set forth in the works which Jesus does. "If I by the spirit of God cast out devils, then is the kingdom of

[4] Gal. 5.22.   [5] 1 Cor. 12.30.   [6] Luke 16.31.

44

God come upon you." [7] "Go, and show John those things which ye do hear and see: the blind receive their sight, the lame walk, the lepers are cleansed, the deaf hear, the dead are raised up, and the poor have the gospel preached to them; and blessed is he whosoever shall not be offended in me." [8] The works declare the range of God's reign as by them Jesus, so to say, wages war against the things in human life which are contrary to it: sickness, maiming, blindness, deafness, disease, possession by devils, mental disorder, hunger. The reign of God is to be a divine order in which these ills are overcome, and the purpose of God is to be supreme in human life, bodily as well as moral, and in nature too. The not infrequent allusions to Old Testament scenes and Old Testament imagery in the miracle narratives connect them with the idea of prophecy fulfilled and the breaking in of the long-expected messianic age. "To-day is the scripture fulfilled in your ears." [9]

Yet emphatically the new order to which the miracles belong is no less an order of righteousness, and none of its mighty works takes precedence before the exposure of sin and the bringing of forgiveness. Intermingled with the episodes of miracle are the episodes of forgiveness and the proclamations of righteousness, and in one arresting story which includes both themes—the story of the paralytic in Mark 2—it is the issue of sin and righteousness which is made paramount. [1] It is this interaction between the works and the righteousness which seems to account for the reserve and the withdrawal which so strangely cut across the healing ministry of Jesus. He cannot allow himself to become merely the popular healer and the purveyor of comfort; to act thus would be to distort the kingdom of God. Hence the withdrawals; and hence too the vigorous pressing home of the righteousness of the kingdom, the need for men to repent and become like little children, the possibility of forgiveness, the calls to renunciation. What are we to infer? The physical benefits of the kingdom are not ends in themselves, but are always subordinate to the divine righteousness. To be healthy, to walk, to hear, to see are not ends

7 Matt. 12.28, cf. Luke 11.20.   8 Matt. 11.4–5, cf. Luke 7.22–3.
9 Luke 4.21.   1 Mark 2.1–12.

in themselves but aspects of a life in which the will of God is done. Just as in our preliminary definition the miraculous is but one fragment of the supernatural, so in the Gospels the works of Jesus are but one fragment of something greater and more elusive: a reign of righteousness reaching beyond the confines of this world.

What happened? The issues of righteousness being paramount the ministry of the works gave place to the journey to Jerusalem to die. "The Son of man must suffer." This was, however, no set-back or defeat, no abandonment of the reign of God. Rather was the death of the Christ on Calvary to be the kingdom's mightiest work of all—as yet. Fulfilling prophecy and forming the basis of a new covenant, the death of Jesus was to be the instrument for the conquest of evil and the coming of the reign in power. Already we almost hear the strains: "Sing my tongue the glorious battle."

Such is the place of the miracles in the story and the teaching of Jesus as the Synoptists present it. Let me add a note by way of an aside. There has been a view that the miracles are to be seen as acts of man, with faith as the key to them, as if to say that Jesus shows that where faith is present, man can subdue nature and conquer pain. What Jesus did all men could do, if only they had faith enough. This was the thesis of a book popular a generation or so ago, D. S. Cairns' *The Faith that Rebels*. On this view I would say only that the connection of the miracles with the humanity of Jesus may be entirely correct. Those who hold him to be divine have no concern to deny that it was in and through humanity and its limitations that the life was lived and the works were done. Yet a close examination of the word *faith* in the synoptic gospels shows, I think, that the faith evoked by Jesus is not a faith in man's power to do miracles or to work cures, but a faith in Jesus as the bringer of the reign of God. It is a response to him, not a response to a belief that man in general could control nature if he had faith enough.

2. Now we turn to the Fourth Gospel. Here at first sight the reader feels a contrast. The reserve and restraint connected with the miracles in the Synoptists seem at first to be absent. The

descriptions of the miraculous seem more stupendous. The evidential motif is more conspicuous, for the miracles avowedly show
forth the glory of the Son of God. "This beginning of signs did
Jesus in Cana of Galilee, and he manifested his glory, and his
disciples believed on him." [2] Yet closer reading considerably modi-
fies the impression of contrast between the Synoptists and John.
There are in John's narrative traces of a restraint which is
eventually to dominate. Twice does Jesus imply that to be im-
pressed by miracles is not the most understanding kind of faith.[3]
And the disciples are perplexed that the manifestation of Jesus
which he predicts beyond the Passion will not be external for the
world to see, but internal to the consciousness of the disciples who
love him.[4] Now the crux about the miracles in the Johannine
story is this. They are indeed evidences of the glory of the Son of
God, but the essence of that glory is deeply ethical—it is the self-
giving love of the Father and Son being wrought out in history.
Hence faith in it is not easy, despite the miracles of Jesus. Just as
in the Synoptists the works belong to a reign of God bound up
with God's righteousness and leading on to the Cross, so in John
the works are part of a glory, bound up with the divine love and
leading on to the Cross as its final manifestation.

It is, however, in his presentation of the works as signs that John
most signally interprets the tradition. In the earlier gospels the
works are not called signs, for "signs" is used of the kind of
vulgar display which people asked for and Jesus deprecated as the
desire of an evil and adulterous generation. Yet the reader of the
story of the feeding of the five thousand easily feels that here is a
symbol of a greater heavenly feeding. And it is hard not to see
symbol in the story, told as it is by St Mark with down-to-earth
factuality, of how blind Bartimaeus, when his eyes had been
opened, sees and follows Jesus *in the way*. John explicitly presents
the miracles as signs disclosing the various aspects of Jesus in his
mission to the human race. He is himself the bread from heaven,
the light of blind humanity, the bringer of life to the dead. The

[2] John 2.11.   [3] Cf. John 4.48; 14.11.   [4] Cf. John 14.22–3.

story of the healing of the man born blind runs on to the terrible climax of the moral blindness of the Pharisees: "because ye say, We see, your sin remains".[5]

To sum up, then, the Gospels present miracles as evidential indeed, but evidential with a very big difference. Their thesis is not: miracles happened therefore Jesus is divine. The miracles partly revealed Jesus for what he is, but partly also baffled because they were bound up with a righteousness and a glory which are seen to involve the Cross. The belief of the disciples first in the messiahship and ultimately in the divine lordship of Jesus was their response to the impact upon them of Jesus himself, and within this impact the miracles had their place as satellites to the sun. The cardinal miracle was and is Jesus himself, for unless the ultimate devotion to him as divine was idolatrous he was a unique breaking of the divine into history and nature. He was the miracle. And the particular miracles showed to those with discerning faith various aspects of his meaning and his claim.

The Resurrection has its own unique significance. It was an event held to be primary and basic for Christianity, inasmuch as without it it is incredible that there could have been the survival of the Church and the emergence of Christianity. Without doubt the apostles used the Resurrection evidentially, as proof of the vindication of Jesus and his claim. We see this in St Peter's speeches in Jerusalem in the early days of the Church. Yet when we look at the evidence by which the apostles themselves were led to believe in the Resurrection we find the reserve characteristic of revelation as we have seen it elsewhere in the New Testament. The evidence which convinced the disciples was evidence visible to none outside their own circle. No evidence was laid before the eyes of the Jews to see. Furthermore, the evidence which convinced the apostles was evidence not wholly separate from their total experience of Jesus, and from their belief in God and in the scriptures. Subsequently, the credibility of the testimony which they gave in their proclamation of the Resurrection was bound

[5] John 9.41.

up with the effect of the event upon their own lives and characters. Thus, in the case of the Resurrection we see the reserve in the evidential process, the inseparability of external evidence from internal experience, and the inseparability of both from the impact of grace upon lives whose character attests their credibility.

III

What of the rôle of historical criticism in relation to the gospel miracles? Did they really happen? If history matters for Christianity, the questions of historical criticism must be faced fairly. It is inevitable to apply historical criticism to the narratives about miracles. When this is done it may be found to be probable that there was at least *some* unhistorical accretion in the miraculous element in the traditions behind the Gospels. For instance it may be that what was originally a parable told by Jesus about the cursing of a fig tree came to be replaced in the tradition of the Church by a story about an actual cursing of a fig tree. It may be that some of the miraculous stories can be given rationalistic explanations. It may be that stories of demonic possession are explicable rather as stories of psychological disorder. All these possibilities must be examined, each in its context. What seems scientifically impossible is to make a dichotomy between the miracles of Jesus and the teaching of Jesus, rejecting the one and accepting the other, for in every part of the gospel traditions sayings and works are inextricably interwoven. No less unscientific is it for historical criticism to take the line that miraculous narratives are to be rejected *a priori*. Such a judgement is not in the sphere of historical criticism: it belongs to other disciplines of thought, and historical criticism confuses its function if it behaves as a philosophy in disguise.

As to the *a priori* question, my reference to it must perforce be brief. Many repeat the proposition that miracles cannot and do not happen because nature is a closed system. It is necessary to examine this proposition, to ask whether nature does not leave room for the operation of free human wills, whether the lawless operation of free human wills has not been responsible for large-scale chaos and frustration, whether God also is not free, whether it is incredible that his freedom should assert itself in the midst of the process of revelation and redemption in the history of Jesus Christ, and whether in this process the breaking by divine freedom of certain normal laws observed in the world may not be regarded as the assertion of some higher law in God's purpose. Those are the questions. I say no more about them than to quote the dictum of St Augustine that miracles may be "non contra naturam, sed contra quam est nota natura",[6] and to quote also the dictum of Archbishop William Temple that to believe in miracle is to take divine personality in real earnest.

Miracle is but one aspect of the supernatural. I suggested that while the concept of the supernatural—call it by what name we will—is an inevitable one, we cannot easily define its boundaries. Baron von Hügel, whom I delight to recall as one of the great Christian thinkers of this century, in his essays on "Heaven and Hell" and on "Christianity and the Supernatural",[7] relates the supernatural specially to phenomena which have an otherworldly reference. But he also insists on the presence of the supernatural not only in experiences avowedly religious but in moral actions anywhere which point to a more than temporal or utilitarian significance for man. The otherworldly reference of the supernatural does not, however, exclude its presence in occasions utterly mundane or trivial where God may be at work for his children's good. He recalls the story of how when Father Faber was dying he was given the last sacraments; but he lived a little longer than was expected, and he asked for the last sacraments again. He was told that he could not have them twice in the same illness, and he then said: "Then let's have another chapter of Pickwick."

None of the good Creator's gifts lie outside the Creator's use of them for his children's good. But this good, lived out as it is in the everyday context of earth, is a good of a more than earthly concern. Down to earth as the supernatural may be, it always relates to a world beyond. So do the miracles recorded in the New

---

[6] *De Civitate Dei* xxi.8.   [7] Cf. *Essays and Addresses* ii. chs. 7, 11.

Testament; not for nothing does one of the apostolic writers call them "the powers of the age to come". So do the people whom Christendom especially calls saints. It so calls them not just because they are good or do good, but because there is in them a humility, an otherworldly touch which help to make God and heaven real and near.

UNITY

Unity, Holiness, and Truth

To-day as we Christian people from every part of the world and from many different traditions meet in New Delhi to work for unity, the supreme fact, towering above all else, is the unceasing intercession of Our Lord. The seventeenth chapter of the Gospel of St John is the utterance, amid the historical crisis of the world's salvation, of a prayer which is everlasting. Our Great High Priest is interceding. And for what does he pray? That his disciples may be one, that they may be sanctified, that they may be sanctified in truth. Unity, holiness, truth; as the prayer is indivisible, so the fulfilment is indivisible too. It is useless to think that we can look for unity in Christ's name unless we are looking no less for holiness in his obedience and for the realization of the truth which he has revealed.

The words of the prayer tell, however, not only of aspirations for the future, but of gifts, once for all given to the Church. By his presence in the Body of which he is the head, he has given to us already unity in himself and in the Father; he has given to us the holiness whose essence is his own self-consecration to his death upon the Cross; and he has given to us the truth which is himself, the very truth incarnate. But it is in the earthen vessels of our frailty that these gifts are ours. Never has there been a moment when the Church has not possessed the gifts, never a moment—since the friction in Jerusalem about widows or in Antioch about eating together or in Corinth about partisanship—when the Church has not obscured the gifts by the sinfulness of its members. In fulfilling its mission the Church has involved itself in the world's life, for its members have always their double citizenship of heaven and earth, their double standing as redeemed sons and members of earthly communities. Hence the Church must needs live out its unity among the changing pressures of culture and polity; it must realize its holiness amid the complexities of successive civilizations; and it must learn and teach its truth amid varieties of intellectual system and method. Small wonder then that amid this involvement truth in the Church has been obscured by human sophistications, holiness has been compromised by worldly pressure, unity has been torn by these causes and many more. All the while the Church shows Christ to the world (for so great is his mercy that he uses the Church mightily despite the failure of its members), and all the while the Church tragically obscures him. But let us get our diagnosis right. Just as our mission is unity, holiness, truth, all three, so our scandal is the distortion of unity, holiness, truth, all three. No less is it in respect of all three that the call comes to our penitence, and our prayer for cleansing and renewal.

The world does not hear the call to holiness, and does not care for the truth in Christ. But the world has its own care for unity, albeit conceived in a secular way; longing for peace it desires that men and nations shall be joined to each other and the forces which separate them removed. And the world, caring thus for unity, is shocked when the Church fails to manifest it. Yet while the world's criticism must rightly humble us, we must not on that account accept the world's conception of the matter. It is not just unity, togetherness with one another, that we seek; and ecclesiastics have sometimes slipped into talking as if it were, isolating unity from the other notes of the Church. It is for unity in truth and holiness that we work and pray, for that is Christ's supernatural gift to us. Let that always be made clear. A movement which concentrates on unity as an isolated concept can mislead the world and mislead us, as indeed would a movement which had the exclusive label of holiness or the exclusive label of truth.

It is when we get back to the depth and comprehensiveness of our Lord's prayer, that we see the depth and comprehensiveness of our quest for unity. What does it include? It includes the ascetical, as well as the intellectual and the diplomatic and ethical. It includes the negotiation of the union of Churches, and of the bringing of Churches into practical fellowship. It includes the task, within them all, of learning the truth in Christ, in scripture in the Fathers, in the liturgies, in contemporary scholarship, in the self-criticism of systems and formulations, a task in which we have been finding ourselves, thank God, rather less like rivals and rather more like fellow-learners. It includes the doing by all of us, and where possible together, of those things which belong to our understanding of Christian conscience, so that even now Christendom may be a reality with an impact and a voice. It includes the ministering to Christ in those who are homeless and hungry. It includes that inner consecration to Christ, in union with his Passion, whereby his holiness is wrought out in us. It includes the constant prayer of Christians everywhere, prayer in which they humble themselves, praying *fiat voluntas*. All this, in depth and breadth, is what the movement to unity must be; and therefore the word "unity" does not suffice to describe it. "I believe in one Church"—we did not learn to say that. We learn to say, "I believe in one, Holy, Catholic, and Apostolic Church," and the notes of the Church are a symphony in depth telling of the depth of Christ's prayer and of the depth of its fulfilment.

Because our task is such, it has both a divine urgency and a divine patience. The call to holiness is urgent; we dare not pray, as did the unregenerate St Augustine, "Lord, give me purity, but not yet". So too is the call to unity urgent. Where there are two or three Christian bodies in a locality, the question urgently presses "why should we not become one?". Yet just as the way of holiness cannot be hurried, and the way of truth cannot be hurried, so too there is concerning unity a divine patience. Guarding ourselves against confusing divine patience and our human sloth, we know that there is a divine patience, to be imitated in our patience with others, in our patience with ourselves, and in our patience with God's age-long patience. Patience includes the will to see that an apparent set-back in some scheme may be our call to go into things more deeply than before. Patience includes, above all, the will to expect that God's blessing upon our own cherished plans may not in his wisdom be separated from his disciplining us in holiness and in truth. We dare not forget the Psalmist's words: "It is good for me that I have been in trouble that I might learn thy statutes." And again, "Thou of very faithfulness hast caused me to be troubled." Patience is needed between those who ask that intercommunion should be immediate and general and those who, with deep conviction and no less concern for unity, think otherwise. We need to remember the moving plea made by Archbishop William Temple at Edinburgh for mutual respect of consciences on this matter.

Within the total task theology has its rôle. We are very conscious of the wounds which we have inflicted upon each other by our theologies, in their corruption. The West has carried to the East not only the Gospel of God, but a score of rival confessional systems which divide those who accept the Gospel; and earlier still the East had its own deadly schisms, in the fourth and fifth centuries, with tragic effects on at least two continents. Hence there is in the West to-day a "hang theology" spirit which says in effect "do not go deep into theology; we need just a few simple facts and principles in order to get unity". But those who talk thus commonly makes themselves large theological assumptions which they do not pause to examine. Beware of them, for if the East cannot find unity in the confessional systems which the West brought to it in an earlier epoch, no more will it find unity in twentieth-century simplifications. Is not the need for West and East to discover those gifts of God which authentically belong not to any one age or phase or culture or continent, but to the one Holy Catholic Apostolic Church of Christ, and to receive them not indeed as a return to any past age but as the media of Christ's dynamic power for the present and the future?

In the realm of theology two good things are happening. One is that within every Church theologians are being inspired by the same interests and are using the same tools. For instance, there is amongst Roman Catholics, Lutherans, Orthodox, Reformed, Anglicans, a kind of concern for the Bible, for the ancient Fathers, and for the liturgy, which is shifting the proportions of thought and teaching and is exposing new levels for converse and partnership. The other is that within our different traditions there is a tendency to put more and more emphasis upon the mystery of God's gracious acts, bringing a deeper humility in men's view of truth and its reception. If we will be patient, true theology, good theology, is something which unites. But it will not be true unless it keeps itself and us near to the Cross whence the call to holiness comes. We need to be humbled in our contentment with our own forms of Christian culture, of intellectual method, of spirituality. We of the West shall try to learn from Asia where new chapters in Christian culture, in intellectual method, in spirituality, are yet to be written.

Unity, truth, holiness; as with the negotiator, so with the theologian, his task is but a tiny fragment. All the while Christ the head of the Church goes on in his mercy using the Church, divided though it be, to make known his truth and unity and to lead many in the way of saintliness. So the divine life of Christ's Resurrection flows in a Church of which the part on earth is but a fragment as it unites us already with the glorious saints in heaven. And all the while our Great High Priest is interceding that in his people unity, truth, and holiness may be seen.

Constantinople and
Canterbury

I count it a great privilege to be the guest of the University of Athens and to be allowed to speak to you as a scholar to scholars. As with so many English scholars my debt to Athens is deep and almost lifelong. It was from the Greek tongue that I learned to love the beauty of words and the meaning of clear thinking. I remember as a boy being told the saying of an English historian of the last century, Sir Henry Maine, "Except the blind forces of nature nothing moves in the world that is not Greek in origin"; and while this dictum is palpably an exaggeration its existence shows how great has been the influence of Greece upon our English culture.

To-night, however, I speak also as a theologian to theologians, as an Anglican to members of the Holy Orthodox Church. In my own Church we cherish primarily the Holy Scriptures as the supreme standard of doctrine, and we believe that nothing may be taught as of necessity for eternal salvation save what may be proved from these scriptures. In the Holy Orthodox Church it is no less evident that the Holy Scriptures are cherished, for whoever studied or expounded the scriptures with more care than the Fathers of the Church? But the Fathers themselves also are cherished by you since you do not sever the Holy Scriptures from the Holy Tradition. He who sees the Holy Orthodox Church from without feels that the ancient Fathers are still alive in you. They are your teachers still, unfolding to you the Scriptures and the mysteries of the faith; and while you have your theologians all down the ages until the present time these bow their heads to the ancient tradition and let the Fathers speak through them.

My own Church has its own history, strangely different from

yours; and the differences are, I cannot doubt, as apparent to you as they are to me. Yet the debt of my Church to the ancient Fathers is very great, and I would speak in the first part of my lecture about the place of the Fathers in our own Anglican theology.

I

Let me remind you of our history. The Church of England was and is a part of Western Christendom. Created partly by Celtic missionaries from Ireland and Scotland and partly by Latin missionaries from Gaul, it was, together with the rest of the West in the early centuries, a part no less of the one undivided Church. We like to remember that one of the great Archbishops of Canterbury, Theodore of Tarsus, who sat in Canterbury's throne from 668 to 693, was a Byzantine Greek, trained in the schools of Athens. Yet of course even then the predominant influences were Western, and after the great schism our English Church was subject to all the influences of the Western Papal Church with which it was bound up. How different was this from the history of your Church of Greece. And how different also from your Church of Greece was it that our Church of England underwent the violent experience of the Reformation in the sixteenth century. Passing through the Reformation our Church was the same Church. We hold that its identity and continuity remained. It still remained, so we believe, the Church of St Augustine and St Theodore of Tarsus; it possessed still the Scriptures, the Creeds, the Sacraments, the mystery of the threefold Apostolic Ministry, the faith of antiquity. But though the same Church, it was a Church reformed. Its communion with the Papal See of Rome was now broken.

Whereas in the East the Holy Tradition had remained in essence the same, in the West the Tradition had been complicated by the accretion of many false traditions in the Middle Ages. It is part of the historical experience of our Church that there had to be rebellion against false "traditions", and when those "traditions" grip tightly the rebellion has to be violent. I beg you to understand this fact in our historical experience. Because there were, for instance, very false ideas about purgatory, the departed, and the saints, there was a tendency of Reformers to depress the meaning of the Communion of Saints unduly. Because there were very false ideas about the Sacrifice of the Mass, it was inevitably hard to grasp at first the conception of Eucharistic Sacrifice in a balanced way. But the Reformation cast aside the false "traditions"; and it did so by asserting the supremacy of Holy Scripture. Side by side with the rejection of the Papal authority this recovery of Holy Scripture was the supreme fact in our English Reformation. The Bible was translated into English; it was put into the hands of the people. It was the guide to the true and primitive faith.

Yet how are the Holy Scriptures to be interpreted? That is a question from which theology cannot escape. It is impossible to interpret them as in a vacuum. It is possible to interpret them in the light of the controversy of a particular age, or in the light of one particular doctrine such as justification or predestination. But from the early years of the reign of Queen Elizabeth, and increasingly in the subsequent reigns, we see in the divines of our reformed Church of England an insistence upon the study of the ancient Fathers as a guide to the understanding of Holy Scripture in the context of the ancient Church.

Archbishop Parker of Canterbury at the Visitation of his Cathedral in 1558 made it an article of inquiry "whether there be a library within this Church, and in the same Augustine's works, Basil, Gregory Nazianzene, Hierome, Ambrose, Chrysostom". In the Canon on preaching issued in 1571 preachers were required to preach only what is found in the Holy Scriptures and "what the Catholic fathers and ancient bishops have collected out of the same". A typical Anglican statement of the respective rôles of scripture and the Fathers is that of Francis White, Bishop successively of Carlisle, Norwich, and Ely. "The Holy Scripture is the fountain and lively spring, containing in all sufficiency and abundance the pure water of life, and whatsoever is necessary to make God's people wise unto salvation. The consentient and unanimous testimony of the true Church of Christ in the primitive ages is *canalis*, a conduit pipe, to derive and convey to succeeding generations the celestial water contained in Holy Scripture. The first of these, namely the Scriptures, is the sovereign authority, and for itself worthy of all acceptation. The latter, namely the voice and testimony of the Primitive Church, is a ministerial and subordinate rule and guide to preserve and direct us in the right understanding of the Scriptures."[1]

We can notice a development in the mode of interest in the ancient Fathers as between the Anglican divines of the reign of Queen Elizabeth and those of the subsequent reigns. In the earlier phase the concern was to use the Fathers as evidence for the primitive faith, to prove that some of the later Roman doctrines were unknown in antiquity. In the later phase, Anglican divines tended to use the Fathers not only for evidence as to what doctrines were, and were not, primitive, but as the medium for their own theological thought and exposition. This was characteristic of the divines of the reigns of Charles I and Charles II, commonly known amongst us as the "Caroline divines". In them we see the appeal to scripture and antiquity, which the Reformers had made, being pursued with maturity, depth, and balance. Their use of the Fathers led them particularly in two directions.

1. They were led away from being preoccupied with the matters which had been the absorbing concern of the Continental Reformers, namely justification and predestination, and became instead influenced by the proportion of the theology of the Fathers for whom the central doctrine was that of the Incarnation of the Word made flesh, the Person of Jesus Christ, God and man. For the Caroline divines, as for the Nicene Age, the Incarnation of the Son of God became the heart and centre of theology. Such was the teaching of the great divines of the Caroline period, such as Lancelot Andrewes and Jeremy Taylor, as it had been the teaching of Richard Hooker in the period before. Such too was the teaching of great divines in the subsequent centuries, William Law and Waterland (different as they were) in the eighteenth

[1] Francis White, *A Treatise of the Sabbath Day* (1635), p. 11.

century; Pusey, Maurice, and Westcott (different as they were) in the nineteenth; Gore and Temple in the twentieth. In every one of these divines the Incarnation was central, and in every one of them the debt to the Fathers was constant and profound.

2. The second trend in the Carolines, caused by their use of the Fathers, was this. Because they found in the Fathers the contrast of Greek and Latin theology they were saved from western narrowness, and were conscious that just as the ancient, undivided Church embraced both East and West so the contemporary Catholic Church was incomplete without the little-known Orthodox Church of the East as well as the familiar Churches of the West, Latin, Reformed, and Anglican. Hence there begins, in the heart of Anglican theology, a yearning towards the East. I quote Lancelot Andrewes, Bishop first of Ely and later of Winchester, whose *Preces Privatae* are a classic work of Anglican devotion. He prayed:

> for the Catholic Church, its development and increase; for the Eastern, its deliverance and union; for the Western, its adjustment and peace; for the British, the supply of what is wanting, the strengthening of what remains in it.

In both these ways the use of the ancient Fathers helped the divines of our English Church to realize in depth, width, and balance the meaning of the appeal to Scripture and Antiquity which our reformers had made. The meaning was this: not only that the Church of England looked back to the undivided Church as a guide or pattern, but that the Church of England claimed to be one with the undivided Church in actual continuity. When our divines saw the Orthodox Church of the East making the claim to be the very Church of the holy apostles, the Church of St Athanasius and St Chrysostom, they believed that they could claim no less for their own Church of England.

You know, of course, that within our Church there have been many varieties of theological type and spiritual outlook, and I am sure that you will understand how our history explains these. There have been those who dwell with exclusive emphasis upon the gifts which the Reformation immediately brought: the supremacy of Holy Scripture and the doctrine that salvation is of God's unmerited gift and not earned by human merits. There have been those who cherish specially the intellectual gifts of the Holy Spirit and delight to relate the Christian faith to contemporary culture. There have been those who most of all cherish the Church's continuity with the undivided Church. Pragmatism is a common English tendency, and often the members of our Church have given themselves to the urgent tasks of Christian duty finding inspiration in the discipleship of Jesus Christ, without a precise concern for theology. The school in our Church which is called Evangelical has been marked specially by the use of the Bible, gratitude to our Lord for his atoning death, the power of the Holy Spirit in personal conviction, and the impulse to win souls to Christ in eager missionary work.

Yet varieties of opinion amongst us have never altered the firm and certain fact that the mysterious life of divine grace and the primitive orthodox faith have continued. The mysteries of Holy Baptism, Confirmation (which is among us not an anointing with oil but a laying on of hands as the sign of spiritual unction), Absolution, Holy Order, Holy Eucharist, Holy Marriage, the Ministration to the Sick (by unction or by laying on of hands) have continued. The Liturgy unites heaven and earth, for Christ once crucified and now risen and glorious is present. The apostolic succession of bishops, priests, and deacons is continued and cherished, and we do not form plans of Church Unity without it. We recite the ancient Creeds in adoration of the Triune God. And God has given gifts of spirituality within our Church beyond our deserving. Not only have these gifts been in the lives of Christian families, fathers, mothers, and children; but there have also been gifts of monastic vocation, with monks, nuns, and friars, who in poverty, chastity, and obedience, serve God both in activity and, like the monks of Mount Athos, in prayer and contemplation. Deeper than the voices of controversy or the Church's many human defects has been this continuity of life, mystical and sacramental. Is this not itself the essence of "holy tradition"?

I mention one more aspect of the Church of England, which belongs specially to the modern phase of its history. It is another example of the influence of the Greek Fathers. The greatest of our modern Anglican divines, such as Bishop Westcott of Durham, Bishop Gore of Oxford, and Archbishop Temple of Canterbury, made the Incarnation the centre of their teaching. But more specially they used the doctrine of the Logos to show that all that is good and true in philosophy, in science, in civilization, is caused by the divine Logos who is at work in all the world as the light that lighteth every man. In the last century the Church in the West was embroiled in the problems caused by modern scientific study. There was the theory of Evolution taught by biologists. There was the rise of historical criticism, with its corollary in the criticism of the Holy Scriptures. There was the rise of new forms of scientific culture. In the midst of this scientific revolution the Church had an anxious task, and I think that this conflict was felt more acutely in the West than in the East. What was the Church to do? It was possible to try to defend the faith as inside an ark, and to regard all science and philosophy outside the Church as an enemy. That was the method of Tertullian. But it was also possible to invoke the doctrine of the Logos as taught most notably by St Irenaeus, and the attitude and temper seen most notably in St Clement of Alexandria. That was the method followed by some notable Anglican theologians, such as Bishop Charles Gore, in facing the new discoveries of science. Using the doctrine of the Logos they were able to show that modern scientific studies are no enemy but have within them the working of the divine Logos who is ever in the world. Such was the task attempted by some modern Anglican divines. Their work could seem strange and modern, and no doubt it could make mistakes; but it was a work at heart orthodox, patristic, Greek in spirit. It is the work of a St Clement in the modern world, just as those who rebuke injustice between classes or races do the work of a St Chrysostom in the modern world.

So our debt to Greece, as Anglicans, haunts us in modern, no less than in older times. Is it surprising that, to borrow the words of the Apostle Paul, we yearn after you in the bowels of Jesus Christ?

II

Now I turn to our tasks of unity. After centuries of division the tide in Christendom flows, however slowly, towards unity and not away from it.

As a man cannot jump out of his own skin or borrow the spectacles of another, I look on the scene inevitably as an Anglican. But the heritage of history causes us as Anglicans to look in many directions, for many forces have pressed upon our history. We remember of course that from the Church of England there has come into existence the widespread family of Churches of the Anglican Communion on every continent, Churches which see in Canterbury an undefined and yet very real symbol of their unity.

We see the Church of Rome. We reject the claim that the Roman Communion is itself the whole Catholic Church in the world, for we cannot deny the claims of the Orthodox Church even before we speak of ourselves and of others too. We reject the adoption of new dogmas as being *de fide* and as binding the faithful. But on a deep level we can learn from the lives and the spiritual teaching of Roman Catholics. We would strive to learn from St Theresa, St John of the Cross, and many others in the life of prayer, and from the self-sacrifice and love of Roman Catholic missionaries. If we are less at home often with Latin scholastic theology we feel kinship with the patristic strain in Roman theology and in the inner life of liturgy. We thank God for the recent awakenings of charity and friendship fostered by His Holiness the Pope. We pray that the forthcoming Vatican Council may serve charity and may serve truth. We do not of course expect the Council to alter the dogmas of the Roman Church. Yet we pray that in proportion and perspective those dogmas may stand out which belong to us also, and which make for peace as Christendom faces the powers of unbelief.

We see the non-episcopal Protestant communions, not least

those which share with us such gifts as the open Bible which the Reformation recovered for us. The unity that we shall, in God's good time, have with them will come through our humility together in the face of God's undeserved gifts to us. These gifts will include the mystery (I use the word of Greek theology) of the ministry handed down to us from the ancient Church. In South India a wonderful act of unity was wrought, and into it many diverse gifts were brought to be joined with those which the Anglican Church has held in trust from the undivided Church. This shows what, under God's hand, is possible. It would be premature to speak now of the discussions which the Church of England is having with the Methodists in England. The Methodists, a movement of spirituality and mission brought into existence by the preaching of John Wesley, were separated when in the eighteenth century the Church of England was cold and formal. There is a great longing for unity, as it was a sad separation. In our striving for unity with the non-episcopal Protestant communions we have to combine the recognition of the divine grace manifested in them with fidelity to that which we have received as having an authority not merely Anglican but Catholic. We have to practise acts of "economy" (to use the Orthodox term) while not obscuring the principles for which we stand.

In Athens, however, it is of the relations of the Anglican Church and the Holy Orthodox Church that I must chiefly speak. Many hearts were stirred by the great conference at Rhodes in September 1961 when the West looked and saw Orthodoxy reasserting its own unity and returning to face the world like a giant refreshed with wine. This rejoiced many hearts. So too did the entrance of more parts of the Holy Orthodox Church, including the Russian Church, into the World Council of Churches at New Delhi in November 1961, and the vigorous participation of the Orthodox there.

I have said enough of our Anglican history to explain why Anglicans have a feeling towards the Orthodox. There is our debt to Greek theology, for Greek theology helped us to discover the meaning of our position and vocation. That debt began before there was more than the smallest personal contact between our Churches. Now that personal contact has become frequent we have come to know Orthodox theology not only as a collection of books but as it is alive in living persons and in the Holy Liturgy. That Liturgy conveys to us the glory of the Resurrection. If in the West we have tended to think of the Liturgy as the infinite condescension of the Lord of Heaven in coming to earth to be the food of our souls, in the East we find that the Liturgy lives and moves in heaven, where Christ is, and the Church is lifted into heaven with him. So too the Liturgy of St Chrysostom makes vivid to us the Communion of Saints. We Anglicans, through the experience of extreme corruption and violent reaction in the West, are hesitant about devotion to the Saints which might even seem to impugn the unique glory of the Son of God, the one Mediator and Saviour. But the Eastern presentation of the Communion of Saints shows the saints not as individual mediators but as members with us and all the departed in the one family of God, and as it is Christ's own glory which is reflected in the saints to honour them is to honour, supremely, him. We see your Church as the Church of the Resurrection, the Church of the Communion of Saints.

If we warm towards you, you have shown warmth indeed towards us. Just over forty-one years ago, in 1920, the Oecumenical Patriarch issued his Encyclical Letter, *Unto all the Churches of Christ wheresoever they be*. To read it now is to see the realism and the prophetic vision which were in it. Three years later, in 1923, the Oecumenical Patriarch declared Anglican orders to be valid in the sense that the orders of Rome and of the Church of Armenia are valid. Grateful for that declaration, we yet realize now—what some were slow to realize—that validity of orders is a thing entirely secondary to agreement in Orthodox Faith. Two years later, in 1925, a remarkable concourse of Orthodox prelates attended the commemoration of the Council of Nicaea in London. Five years after that, in 1930, there met in London the Anglican and Orthodox theological commission. Its Report, issued in 1931, is a fine analysis of the theological issues. In 1935 there came the conference in Bucharest between the Church of England and the Church of Roumania, and the valuable report which came from it. The war disturbed these growing relations, and prevented contacts. Since the war there was in 1956 the conference in Moscow in which is was my privilege to lead the Anglican delegation in discussion with representatives of the Patriarch of All Russia. Today I am, like my predecessor in 1960, on my way home from receiving the gracious hospitality of the Oecumenical Patriarch.

Let me dare to suggest some considerations which seem to me important in our coming theological task, not forgetting that the theological task is blended with the work of practical relations and spirituality.

1. I plead that in all our discussion justice is done to those differences of historical circumstance which condition our theological expression. Take for instance the question of the *filioque* clause which the West inserted into the Niceno-Constantinopolitan Creed. Inevitably the Orthodox Church resents the insertion of a clause into the Creed. But let it be explained that when we of the West say the *filioque* we have no intention of asserting that there is more than one αἰτία or πηγή (I use your Greek terms) in the Godhead, and that the *filioque* was valued in order simply to uphold the *homoousion* amid controversies in the West which you in the East did not experience. Take also some of the phrases in our Thirty-nine Articles; these phrases result from the necessity of rejecting certain corrupt doctrines which had no equivalent in Eastern history. We need to examine the historical circumstances in order to have mutual understanding.

2. The question of Holy Scripture and Holy Tradition looms large in our discussions. I believe that the Holy Tradition is living in our Church; for what is Holy Tradition but the continuous stream of divine life, which is the very life of God Incarnate and of the Holy Spirit within the Church? This divine life is in the scriptures, the preaching of the Gospel, the Sacraments, the lives of Christians, the fellowship of the Saints. Such is the Holy Tradition. In our Anglican theology we do not speak of it precisely as you do. But it is there, with us and in us. We ascribe to Holy

Scripture a supreme right to check and test what properly belongs to Holy Tradition and what does not. Here perhaps is a path along which we may move towards understanding.

3. We Anglicans realize that you Orthodox see Orthodoxy as something one and indivisible, one indivisible plentitude of faith, worship, and customs. It is like a beautiful picture. If even a small smudge is cast upon the picture, or one small injury done to it, the *whole* picture is spoilt. I think that this is perhaps the biggest difficulty of all in some of our theological discussions. It concerns the *nature* of Orthodoxy, and the way of accepting it. Here, I think that we need to give thought to the relation between the Church as eternal and the Church as embodied in the movement of history, and also to the relation between divine Truth and the words in which divine truth is embodied. This latter question is not a new one created by modern desires for lack of precision: it is an old question with which some of the Fathers were concerned. I recall words of St Hilary, "We are compelled to attempt what is unattainable, to climb where we cannot reach, to speak what we cannot utter. Instead of the bare adoration of faith, we are compelled to entrust the deep things of religion to the perils of human expression." [2]

I modestly suggest these few considerations for the future of our theological task, the task to which theologians, Orthodox and Anglican, are together called. It is a task which bears not only upon our own Church relations but upon the general problem of Christian Unity—for what might not be the wider effects of a growing unity between our Churches of East and West? Theological work, prayer, liturgy, friendship, and action together to meet the world's distresses, all these are part of the way to unity. The Holy Tradition is God Incarnate living and moving in the whole life of Christians.

III

While we discuss the theology and the church life of Constantinople, Canterbury, and Rome too, there is around us the modern

[2] *De Trinitate* II. 2.4.

world wherein is terrible rejection of divine truth and indifference to it. The task of unity among ourselves is inseparable from our bringing the Everlasting Gospel of God to the nations. No less necessary is it for the Church to meet the contemporary scientific culture, and to go out to succour those who are in hardship and distress.

1. There is the presence in the world of a modern, scientific, technological culture, so different from the older culture of Athens, or Oxford or Cambridge. Can our theology ignore this scientific culture? I can think of theologies whose nature it would be to say, "Yes, we can ignore it". But such is not the nature of Greek theology or of Anglican, wherever the Greek spirit has influenced it. The divine Logos, working in all the created world, the author of all truth, the inspirer of all knowledge properly so called, is working within the scientific methods of our time. If we shrink from saying this we may be in danger of being false to the teaching of the Fathers. If we do say this, then theologians will be conversing not only with one another in the ecumenical exchange but with every sort of other academic discipline, not least those which seem most modern. The theologian will best teach when he is ready to learn and to receive wherever the Divine Wisdom is the teacher.

2. There is the distress of nations through poverty and hunger, and the distress of races through the lack of brotherhood between them. Here we can listen again to the prophetic words of St Chrysostom that it is vain to come to the altar in the Eucharist unless we go out to find the altar which is identical with the poor brother: "This altar thou mayest see everywhere lying both in lanes and market-places, and thou mayest sacrifice upon it every hour. When thou seest a poor brother reflect that thou beholdest an altar." [3] St Chrysostom knew the very rich and the very poor within his own city. To-day there are countries relatively prosperous and countries of deep poverty. The succour of the homeless and the refugees is a very part of our search for unity in Christ.

[3] Homily XX, on 1 Corinthians.

The Church of God will therefore go out both to learn and to use whatever the divine wisdom discloses in the modern world, and to meet the agonies which are in the world. It can do this with conviction, because it knows the truth about the world and the truth about itself. The *world* is a place where Christ by his death and resurrection has won a cosmic victory: it is in his hands already, and all unseen his power draws it into unity: that is the orthodox Faith of Christ Victorious, as the Fathers and the Liturgy attest. The *Church* is a body where, amidst its many sinful and fallible members, Christ is present as the Church's inward life; and the portion of the Church on earth is ever one with the Church in paradise and heaven.

Anglicans
and the Future

O God, thou art my God: early will I seek thee.

Ps. 63.1

In our act of worship to-night we proclaim once again that the adoration of God is the first privilege and the final goal of us his creatures and children. The claim that worship comes first rests upon the elementary fact that God created us in his own image after his own likeness, and longs that we shall have with him the closest fellowship possible in love and in converse, a love and converse intimate and yet filled with awe and dependence as God is our Maker as well as our Father. He made us for himself, and our heart is restless until it find rest in him.

Beneath the strains and agonies of our modern world there lies the estrangement of Man from his Creator. In the midst of such a world as this the Church of God bears witness to the truth about God and Man as Jesus Christ has finally disclosed it, and in no way does the Church do so more significantly than in the depth of its worship. "O God, thou art my God, early will I seek thee." An unknown Christian writer of old wrote, "as the soul is in the body, so are the Christians in the world". By lifting up their souls in the simplicity of love towards God Christians are doing on the world's behalf what the world has lost the power to do, and they are serving the world by helping it to recover the soul which it has lost. To say this is no platitude. Rather is it a priority which the Church is all too ready to neglect. In the noise of our times there is little enough of the quiet waiting upon God which is the heart of our religion. In the activism of our Church life there is a forgetfulness that the reality of God is not necessarily made known by the multiplying of the things we do. We need to be recalled to St Dominic's great description of the Christian way: *"contemplare et contemplata aliis tradere"*, to contemplate and to pass on to others the things contemplated. Is our weakness in the second due to our being often too busy for the first?

It is, however, in no vacuum that God is worshipped. As our Lord's going to the Father was bound up with his loving identification of himself with humanity ravaged by sin and suffering, so the Church's offering of its life to God is bound up with its mission to humanity. As with Christ, so with the Church, it is an obedience set within place and within time. Christ's obedience was on the soil of Palestine, and in the time of Pontius Pilate the Governor. So our obedience is always in a place, and always in a time. *Place:* the Church serves God in the heart of particular countries, cultures, languages, making itself in the people, of the people as it does so. It must be in turn as Canadian as the Canadians, as African as the Africans, as Asian as the Asians. *Time:* we remember that in the New Testament "time" is a terrible word, sharp as a knife. It is καιρός: time urgent in opportunity and in judgement. It is less often the year or the day than the hour or the minute, each hour, each minute being a *time* of visitation: evening, midnight, cockcrow, morning, the Lord may come. We may be leisurely studying an era, when the divine hour or moment passes and finds us asleep and does not come back again. Yes, it is in places and in times that our love for God is tested. "O God, thou art my God, *early* will I seek thee."

To-day's gathering here in Toronto finds us all belonging to geography, to our homes and countries far distant from one another, and belonging to time, to the mid-twentieth century. But we serve God in geography and in time only because we have a citizenship which is beyond both of them. Think how this is so.

Beyond locality, every one of our churches, provinces, dioceses is a part of the one Holy Catholic Church of Christ. From that, in Christ, each part derives its strength. Towards that, in Christ, each part looks away from itself in realizing its mission. Integrated with the one Catholic Church in baptism, liturgy, creed, apostolic order, we share in a stream of divine life and truth at once outward and visible and deeply interior as well. Wherever there is full communion there is the unhindered sharing in both the interior and the visible unity. It is this which our Orthodox friends call "the holy tradition". And while our life in Christ is thus a life beyond geographical regions, so too is our mission. As the world becomes smaller by the involvement of every part with every part, so we cannot serve this or that portion of humanity without our togetherness in serving all.

Beyond time, our own generation of Christians belongs to a Communion of Saints reaching across the generations. Time seems to disappear as we find our family union with saints and martyrs of old, with the apostles, with the Mother of Our Lord. Let us realize more vividly the Communion of Saints in the bond of prayer and eucharist, and let us be sure that to do so is not to be merely looking backwards in history but rather to be looking onwards towards the vision of God in heaven as, in fellowship with the saints who are nearer to that vision, we say "O God, thou art my God, early will I seek thee".

So it is that serving God *here* or *there* we know our part in the great Church beyond here and there, and serving God *now* or *then* we know our share in the Communion of Saints in which before and after melt into one another. Within this setting there is our own Anglican Communion. It is here that our lot is cast, it is here that God's providence has put us. And we ask what this means for us, and what it should mean for Christendom. In a word, I suggest, it means this. The Anglican Communion is the medium whereby while serving in this country or that country we know our place within the one Holy Catholic Church, and while serving here and now we know our place within a stream of providential history.

Thus, while we are striving that the Church we serve shall be as Canadian as the Canadians, as African as the Africans, as Asian as the Asians, it is in our Anglican Communion that we know our wider catholicity, not just ideally or invisibly or federally, but in the sacramental depth of full communion and in practical fellowship. In this fellowship we witness together to a faith and a sacramental life scriptural and catholic. The providences of history have brought this about. Ours is a continuity in history, in catholicity, in mission, with the mission of St Augustine from Gaul to England, when he built his church and set his chair in Canterbury. We owe much to Rome at whose behest that mission happened. With Constantinople we are one in things deeper than the differences brought about by our very diverse historical experiences. So too our debt to Geneva is great, for Geneva helped us and helps us still to know that all is by grace alone and by faith alone. This history is not a bare history. It is a history with a meaning. It passes through localities like the Isle of Thanet and the gates of Canterbury. But the meaning is more than local. Not for nothing do the Anglican chaplaincies on the continent call themselves "Canterbury houses" or "Canterbury clubs". Not for nothing do you come in thousands as pilgrims to Canterbury. Set as she is in a corner of the island she is a symbol of our widespread brotherhood, a brotherhood in which we all serve one another as we serve Christ and the world.

It is not for us Anglicans to speak in self-consciousness or self-commendation about our claims. There was a period when other Churches used to speak nice complimentary words about our rôle as a "bridge-Church". To-day in an ecumenical age Christians everywhere are ready to go to one another without the aid of our bridge, or perhaps any bridge to help them. We learn again that self-consciousness and self-commendation have no place in Christ. Yet God gives us a quiet assurance of faith, and in the quiet assurance of faith we look towards the world, towards one another as Anglicans, towards other Churches, and towards God. As a new epoch in Christian history may be opening we ask where our task and our duty are going to be.

Towards the world we renew our mission. It will be more than ever a mission of involvement—as Canadian as the Canadians, as African as the Africans, as Asian as the Asians. Involved with the growing nations we shall be no less involved with the religions, acknowledging the light that lighteth every man present among them while we proclaim Christ as the unique Saviour, light of light. No less shall we be involved with the great mass of modern secularism, putting ourselves with sympathy and sensitivity along-side every groping towards God while always adhering to a supernatural faith. In all these ways our mission will be one of involvement, but we know that the power to fulfil it will go with the Church's otherworldly witness.

Towards one another as Anglicans our unity will be one of giving and receiving. We must plan our mission together, and use our resources in the service of our single task. The word missionary will mean not colonialism of any kind, but all of us going to one another to help one another. Let African and Asian missionaries come to England to help to convert the post-Christian heathenism in our country and to convert our English Church to a closer following of Christ.

Towards other Churches we work for unity in truth and holi-ness. That work is always one of giving and receiving, and we only give if we are humble to receive. What we may give is not our own, it is a treasure of scriptural and catholic faith and sacra-ment. As to the goal, it is nothing less than full communion in and of the Catholic Church of Christ. In the process parts of the Anglican family may cease to be precisely Anglican, as united Churches come into being in full communion with us. But whether our Anglican Communion itself will disappear is some-thing which we do not know. We do not know what place par-ticular provinces or traditions or patriarchates will have within the unity of God's design, and Canterbury may, like Rome and Constantinople, long have its rôle in God's service. Meanwhile the work of unity has its times, its καιροί, in different parts of the world. For all of us there is in this year the great significance of the Vatican Council. Rome and Canterbury are speaking to one another in a new charity without belittling their respective con-cerns about truth. And though the road to unity in truth is a long one, the new charity means that already Christendom stands more vividly as a fact before the world.

"O God, thou art my God, early will I seek thee." To him we turn, first and last, and only as we do so can we with any purpose turn towards the world, towards one another, and towards other Churches. To contemplate, and to pass on to others the things contemplated, that is always the order; and we make God known only when we have ourselves been humbled by the vision of him. It is in the vision of him that he increases and self decreases; and those who know us may find less of ourselves and more of God. "Early will I seek thee", says the Psalmist, and our Lord answers, "Seek, and ye shall find".

THE
CONTEMPORARY
WORLD

Christian Responsibility
in a World Society

This is a conference[1] of Christian men and women who are determined to see the world and its problems in the light of the Christian hope. Throughout the centuries the Christian hope has been regarded in two ways. We may dwell upon the hope of heaven, and heaven is the fulfilment of the design of the Creator that those whom he has made in his own image will come to perfect fellowship with him and to the vision of him for ever. We may dwell upon the coming of the kingdom of God upon earth, the vindication of God's purpose here in time and history. But neither aspect of the Christian life is tenable without regard to the other. On the one hand we cannot conceive the coming of God's kingdom in the world apart from the consummation in heaven. On the other hand as we look towards the vision of God in heaven, we know that just because heaven is the perfection of love we do not advance one step towards heaven unless the same love is showing itself in our service of the human race here and now and in our healing of its wounds and divisions.

This double aspect of the Christian code determines our attitude towards the state, the nation, and the individual man and woman. The *State* has a God-given rôle for the provision of order, justice, and the well-being of a nation; but though the State will pass away, its citizens are creatures in God's image with our eternal destiny, and the State understands its duty to them only if it knows that they have a heavenly goal bound up with absolutes of right and wrong. The *Nation* has a God-given rôle, understood aright not only as the fulfilment of its own corporate life, physical and spiritual, but as its service of the other nations; the scene of Christ

[1] Held by the Wyndham Place Trust, 15 November 1962.

washing the feet of the disciples is to be imitated not only by individuals but by communities and nations in their service of one another. The *individual* has his vocation here within state and nation, a vocation both to self-fulfilment and to service, and at every moment this vocation is affected by his eternal status. Yes, this double aspect of our life is perplexing to those outside the Christian tradition, and in its practical applications it is often perplexing to ourselves. Yet it alone gives the real answer to Communism or self-centred nationalism or a merely material view of progress, and it gives us the starting-point for any Christian consideration of our present duty.

I ask now how these principles bear upon some of the questions with which to-day's conference is going to be concerned.

1. First, the Christian will, as the outcome of the doctrines which I have been describing, want his country to be the servant and the helper of other countries. He will be concerned to see his country doing all it can for the help of the impoverished peoples, especially those where hunger is acute. He will want to emphasize that if his country enters a group of nations, say a European group, for their mutual benefit there must be the utmost concern at the same time for the help of the underdeveloped and poor countries.

2. Next, the Christian, knowing that human fulfilment is bound up with obedience to divine love will watch carefully the concept of freedom and the claims made for it. The "free world" does not properly mean just a group of nations with democratic institutions or a group of nations which have escaped the Communist yoke. The freedom with which Christians are concerned is achieved not just by democratic institutions, but by democratic institutions disciplined by the highest ideals. And freedom cannot be defended by building a rampart around it. It survives by its power to give itself creatively to nations which lack it, a giving which will include both things material and things spiritual. It is thus that the West must look towards Africa and Asia, and give of its best to them while there is yet time.

3. Thirdly, the Christian will be concerned that, just as his

nation serves other nations, so too his state will be bound by sanctions beyond itself. Here we touch the crux of to-day's Conference, and the crux of the present international problem; the crux is the question of the limits of sovereignty. It is not a new problem. Sovereignty has been limited in the past when states have bound themselves by treaty to act in such and such a way in face of an aggressive war against an ally or a member of a league. In the first phase the limitation was not a deference to an institution with authority but a deference to a moral covenant felt to be binding. In the transitional phase the limitation is not merely a deference to a covenant but a deference to a league of nations, an organism of states empowered by its members to call upon them to take certain actions. How far do we now go? That is now the question pressing upon us. Are we ready not only to affirm a limit to the sovereignty of states by their obligations to the group which has covenanted together, but also to support a force of policemen who will act, in the name not of this state or of that state but of this new entity above them, whose claim to act in the name of justice they recognize?

It is here that Christian people without knowing all the answers can give help and leadership. We may not yet know how in theory this new entity is to be defined in relation to national sovereignties. But we do know that national sovereignty has limits; this has been a Christian assertion from the beginning. And we do know that if a man wills to do the will of God he shall know the doctrine whether it be of God. It is in that faith that Christian people can support such a project as an international force, not just by voting for it but by giving the service of lives to it. And, as so often in the past, the adventure of faith leads on to the finding of the answer to the theoretic questions: in this case the question of exactly how far, and exactly by what, must the sovereignty of states be limited.

I offer therefore to the Conference this attempt to state some principles upon which Christians may stand, and some contemporary applications of them, in the belief that in so far as the applications are carried out with faith and courage the principles themselves will come to be seen with greater clarity, and vision will be given to formulate them more fully. But let me end where I began with the twofold aspect of the Christian hope.

To-day any nation or group, any Church or individual, feels at times helpless amid the violence of the world and the intractability of human affairs. What can we do? Does anything that we do really signify? We answer, from the one side of the Christian hope, that every single act of charity or justice has its part in that training of souls for eternity which is the Creator's first and final purpose for human beings. We answer also, from the other side of the Christian hope, that every single act of charity or justice witnesses to the supreme worth of the individual man and woman in this world and serves, even though we may not quite see how, the victory of our Creator's purpose here on earth.

Sex and Civilization

The death of Lord Samuel will have sent those who admired him to recall some of his finest utterances as statesman and philosopher, and not a few will remember the speech in the House of Lords nearly ten years ago[1] when he spoke of how "the moral state of the nation is at the base of everything else, and in these days there is, among careful watchers of the times, a feeling of deep anxiety". Among the moral issues was one about which Samuel had written these prophetic words sixteen years earlier:

It seems likely that in this matter of the family, there will develop two contrasted schools of thought, each, as time goes on, defining more and more clearly its own philosophy. The one will lay stress upon freedom, self-satisfaction, enjoyment; will treat sexual relationships lightly; will regard a marriage as experimental, will prefer to be childless or to have one child or two, and will look upon children's interests as secondary. The other school will lay stress upon lasting affection, stability, the home, children, the family system. They will regard the permanency of marriage as a matter of course. Their own matrimonial differences they will resolve, because they hold that they must be resolved. . . .

In between the two schools there will be many gradations; but fundamentally there are those opposite philosophies, and the world must choose between them.[2]

I would make at once one qualification in Lord Samuel's antithesis. There are not only the adherents and the practitioners of these two creeds. There are also those who would fain follow the path of the Jewish and Christian ideal, but have been made casualties amid the society we live in. I make the point here and

[1] 4 November 1953.   [2] *Belief and Action*, Pelican edn., p. 130.

now because the Christian Church is often (wrongly) regarded as showing only harshness to the divorced. But both to the wronged and to the wrong there must ever be offered Christ's compassion, and the power to re-create good from out of ill.

To-day society is not less, but more, like the words of the statesman's warning. Sexual morality is in a mess. Some would say at once that the reason is the decline of religious belief and sanction, since it is with that belief and sanction that morality has been bound up. Others would say that on the contrary this belief and sanction had been the cause of false repression, neurosis, and unhappiness, and that the contemporary revolt was freeing sex to be the happy, carefree, innocent delight it was meant to be, and was pointing the way to new moral insights. Here the Christian has to make his response. It is not enough to point to a tradition or to assert an authority. Christian morality is to be *commended* to reason and conscience. We need, while abhorring evil, to try to analyse where the evil lies, and what are the causes which make for it. That is my purpose in this article.

The debris of bad apologetics, false images, and narrow moralism must be cleared away. The Christian ethic is not primarily a set of rules and prohibitions: "Thou shalt", "Thou shalt not". It is not an isolated concentration upon sex, as if fornication were the only grave sin, and chastity the paramount virtue. It is not, again, a hush-hush smugness which cannot talk of sex and leaves it to be deemed unclean or smutty. Nor is it a thing called "sex ethics", invoked to counteract "sex licence"; for the essence of the Christian view is that sex is to be understood only in the context of the whole relation of man and woman.

What are the facts and principles upon which monogamy rests? Male and female, the difference of gender belongs to many parts of nature as well as to humanity. It links humanity with nature, and also serves humanity's divine goal which reaches far beyond it. The delicate division of gifts and qualities leaves man eager for woman, and woman eager for man. Eros, or love, is the desire of the one for the other, as the one feels incomplete without the other; it is a desire to possess and to be possessed. Venus is the pleasurable act in which union is expressed and deepened; it serves Eros and Eros craves for it.

But Eros and Venus together do not exhaust the meaning of man and woman in their togetherness. Man and woman are selves, they are persons; they bring to one another a wealth of thoughts, actions, interests, concerns, and these are to become the stuff of the unity between them, without individuality disappearing. What monogamy does is not only to unite Eros and Venus to one another but to unite them both with the whole realm of unities in which man and woman can be joined. Thus it is that these are linked with *Philia*, the whole range of comradeship in life together with all that this involves. And as God is the giver and God is the goal, there comes also within the relation of man and woman the *Agapé* which is the divine self-giving kind of love without which the rest may go astray.

Such is monogamy. Its emergence in history, its interior depth, and its stable continuance require the sacrifice of a great restraint: that Venus is not indulged outside the marriage bond and that Venus is not indulged before it. Marriage to-day, whether in church or registry, is a contract to accept a lifelong bond; and through it a man and a woman enter upon not just a series of activities together but a *status*. It is in terms of *status*—husband, wife, father, mother, children—that monogamy serves the security of society as well as the divine goal for humanity.

To-day there is in our society an immense outbreak of pre-occupation with Venus. There is a dwelling upon sex: the sex problem, the adjustments of sex, instruction for sex, adventures of sex, stories of sex, what to do with sex, brighter and better sex. How has this come about? In the frustrations of our society that inner unity between Venus, Eros, Agapé, and the other factors in the true unity of man and woman has been torn apart. But just as the uprush of sexuality in the decaying Graeco-Roman world was not due to sex impulses in themselves but to frustrations which caused men and women to turn to sex as an escape, so does it seem to be to-day.

It is not that the native impulses of sex are stronger, or that

men and women are more lustful. Rather is it that the many
frustrations which beset people, their insecurities, their want of
fulfilment, their lack of meaningfulness in work or home or
human relations, their lack of significance for the *ego*—these drive
them to find in Venus a realm where they can succeed. In the
adventures and sensations of Venus there is the chance to achieve,
to dominate, to win, to enjoy, to prove oneself to oneself and to
others. The adventures are not always merely lustful; some of
them, however wrong and mistaken, are adventures in personal
giving and receiving, in searches for fulfilment. But if society's
frustrations create the preoccupations with Venus, it in turn
deepens and extends those frustrations.

Hence Venus looms large. And with the preoccupation some
great misunderstandings follow. One is that Venus is itself the
substance of marriage, and the clue to its success. It is assumed in
much popular, and even in some "scientific" literature that success
or failure in marriage is concentrated in the realm of Venus; but
the fact is that breakdown in marriage is often in the realm of
character, patience, forbearance in living together, and disturb-
ances *there* are reflected in the physical difficulties.

So, too, is it assumed by many that as the art of marriage will
be the art of Venus *in excelsis*, therefore the best readiness for
marriage will be a training in sexual experience and techniques.
This assumption helps to encourage the widespread increase of
pre-nuptial unchastity. There comes the tragic fallacy that the
spread of pre-matrimonial sexual experience makes for better and
happier marriages. In truth, this misconceives the nature of the
marriage relationship and increases in society the severance of the
elements from which that relationship is made.

This, however, can be said of the contemporary preoccupation
with sex. Linked as it is with frustrations and distortions in life as
a whole it is in large part of a mental preoccupation due to a
pervasive kind of mental conditioning. It is not that the power of
Venus to allure men and women is stronger than it was. Rather is
it that our distorted mentality has piled upon Venus a load greater

than she can properly bear, and has given to her a rôle far beyond that which she was created to fulfil.

Lord Samuel was right. The "deep anxiety" of which he spoke remains, and so does the abhorrence of evil. I have tried to analyse some aspects of contemporary evil, for it is on a right analysis that the answer must be based. It is an answer which involves not only the true understanding of sex, but the motives, the ends, and the pattern of our civilization, and the rôle of home and family, men and women within it. Here is the task to which Christians are called to address themselves.

The Laws of Divorce

My Lords, it is known to everyone that the Churches have definite beliefs about marriage and divorce, and it has been suggested (though not here to-day) that there is a wish on the part of churchmen to impose those beliefs upon the law of the country. The truth is this. While the Churches have their beliefs and standards which they urge their members to follow and teach that they can follow by the help of God's grace, they accept the fact that a great many citizens do not share their beliefs and that this is reflected in the divorce laws of the country. The Churches are, however, concerned with what is likely to be good and right for the country as a whole, and it is from that concern that I for one express my views about the legislation now before us.

My Lords, we have the problem now before us because there is something very wrong in the country, and this has been growing. Too many marriages break down, there are too many strains in families, too many illicit unions both before and after marriage. Why is this? It is because of the many tensions about sex and marriage to which so many people, especially perhaps young people, are liable. I welcome wholeheartedly the greater openness about sex which exists to-day, as sex can be a good and beautiful thing and the wrong kind of hush-hush attitude about it can do harm. Yet there is in much of the population a preoccupation with sex, a lack of discipline about it, and so many temptations to incontinence on all sides—especially as the physical dangers of incontinence seem not to be so great as they once were. Hence the background from which marriage is approached by many people is a confused one, and too many couples enter marriage with the scales already weighted against their making it a life-long success. The status of marriage is undermined in the minds of so many of the people, and because its status is undermined the tendency increases for couples to approach it without enough understanding and dedication to its meaning.

That is the background to our questions about divorce, and I would urge that while we should view this question with great sympathy for those in hardship through broken marriages we should also view it from the angle of the status of marriage for those who approach it.

So I come to the clause which has been moved by the noble Lord, Lord Silkin. The plea is made that it will remove hardship from many whose marriages have broken down, and that it will remove hardship from children at present illegitimate. These are important pleas, and I will come back to them, because it is impossible not to have sympathy with distress of any sort. But I would plead that we consider this other question: What effect will the clause have upon the status of marriage, its essential meaning and definition for those who approach it or are trained for it? This is a grave question. Divorce after seven years' separation, if there is no consent, can involve injustice; and if it is a matter of consent, it alters by reflex implication the meaning of the marriage covenant. It makes the words, "till death us do part", mean in effect "until we decide that we are tired of one another, and agree to end it". At present both the church marriage and the registry marriage state and imply the intention by the parties to enter a life-long covenant. It will be very hard to say that this is really so if the principle of this new clause is established.

But, my Lords, what is said on the other side? It is said that at present people whose marriages are broken are driven to commit a matrimonial offence in order to get a divorce. This is sometimes true, and it is an evil state of affairs. But I think that the alternative proposal is a greater evil, namely that with the necessity of specific offence put on one side there is created an honourable, respectable way of ending a marriage, namely by separation or consent. I agree with the nine members of the Royal Commission who said: "There can be no more subtle temptation to divorce than the belief that there is a wholly blameless way of ending a marriage." Again, it is said that the passing of this clause will bring to an end a number of illicit unions. It will indeed turn a number of what are now illicit unions into second marriages and happy ones too. I appreciate that. But will it reduce the number of illicit unions which come into existence? No, my Lords, that would seem very improbable. The availability of this new ground for divorce will not deter people from entering into illicit unions, for people will be encouraged to do so, secure in the knowledge that after the statutory number of years they would be free to marry. It would also facilitate the designs of a person who had no scruple about breaking up someone else's marriage. If a woman wants to entice a husband away from his wife, she would be in a stronger position to do so under this new clause as she would know that eventually a divorce could be forced upon the innocent wife; and that is perhaps the most alarming of the new possibilities which the clause would create.

I believe, my Lords, that these considerations weigh against the rightness of this clause.

I refer now to the plea on behalf of illegitimate children who would, if the clause were passed, have the chance of becoming the legitimate children of a married home through their father marrying their mother. Yes. But this would be at the expense of the father's first partner and the children of the first (and married) union. The easier you make it for the second woman to become regularly married to a man, the more likely she is to take the risk of living with that man until she can be married to him. It is not at all unlikely that *more* people would be injured by the operation of this new ground for divorce than would be helped by it. Is it right to try to legitimize children by divorcing someone else?

I have now set out the case against this clause as I see it. In a letter in *The Times* yesterday Mr Abse asked whether the case of churchmen who oppose the clause was based only on dogma or on sociological considerations. I would say that the considerations which I have been putting to your Lordships are sociological considerations; they concern the deep well-being of society.

As to dogma it is a word which arouses prejudice, so let me use

94

the word "belief". The Churches are not asking to impose their belief on those who do not accept it, for churchmen have already accepted that there is a divergence between their belief and the State's laws of divorce. But other people besides Churches have beliefs, and there is still some common ground between them; and it is a great gain for the country that wherever a marriage is conducted it is affirmed to be a life-long covenant. We have our terrible problems largely because the status of marriage is weakened and the approach of so many people to it is wrong. Do not, my Lords, weaken this status further. Do not, out of motives of compassion which all of us feel, cut at the ground of compassion itself: do not meet the hardships of some in such a way as to weaken the security of the many.

My Lords, this is not to say that I am content with the present law of divorce and operation of the divorce courts. When the recent statement by a number of Church leaders ended with the words, "we are anxious to examine any measures for reducing hardships which would not sap the foundation of marriage", we meant what we said. It is very hard to see what can be done, but I am concerned that we should try. Is it not worth while asking for further examination of the word "illegitimate"? Is it necessary that for all purposes, for example bequests, there should be the present distinction at all? If it were possible to find a principle and a law of breakdown of marriage which was free from any trace of the idea of consent, which conserved the point that offences and not only wishes are the basis of the breakdown, and which was protected by a far more thorough insistence on reconciliation procedure first, then I would wish to consider it. Indeed, I am asking some of my fellow churchmen to work at this idea, sociologically as well as doctrinally, to see if anything can be produced. In Belgium there is a provision for what the law of that country calls "divorce by mutual consent" which I have been studying. But the procedure is so hedged about by stage upon stage of reconciliation procedure that it is very far removed from "divorce by mutual consent" as we understand it in our discussions in this country; indeed, I wonder whether for our purposes the title of the Belgian procedure does not rather mislead.

Let us, my Lords, examine every possibility of helping the illegitimate, and of improving our divorce laws. But let us not undermine what is not only the belief of the Churches but the meaning of marriage as one of the bases of our society.

The Robbins Report

My Lords, my own interest in this important subject is coloured by the fact that I was for a good many years a university teacher, and my experience included both an ancient and a modern university. I learned to admire the virtues of both and to see some of the difficulties of both. Were I still in academic life I am sure that I should be looking forward to exciting possibilities in view as a result of the Robbins Report, and I join in the tributes to it as a remarkable document. Public discussion of it has been chiefly around the question, Will the quality of university standards be maintained amidst an increase of the university population by 40% in the next three years and by three times by the year 1980? The Report argues that the standards can be maintained since the increase of university population will bring with it the necessary increase of teachers, research workers, and good scholars. But it argues the case with no sort of complacency, and makes and implies some important caveats: that there must be special efforts to safeguard research, to secure the right balance between broad courses and specialized courses of study, that there must be good tutorial methods developed with the right sort of contact between teachers and students, and above all that two-thirds of the expansion must be residential. My fear is that the policy of expansion may go forward, and that the important caveats may not be safeguarded as they should be, for pressure of expansion or for economic reasons. I much regret the suggestion that the policy of two-thirds of the increased university population being residential might not be insisted upon on the ground that the best can be the enemy of the good. If compromises like that are made we may get neither the good nor the best but the worst in academic development.

Now, my Lords, I am not sure that the Robbins Report goes

deeply enough into what the quality of good standards really means. It describes the chief elements in good standards well enough: the needs of research, the varieties in the kinds of good teacher, the value of tutorial work, of residence, and so forth. But I believe that the secret of a good university lies not just in those elements existing in requisite quantities, but in a community wherein they are interrelated one to another in a certain undefinable genius.

Mr X or Mr Y enters a university, whether Oxbridge or Redbrick or some species yet to be invented. What does he expect? To be trained for his profession or taken a long part of the way towards it? Yes. Yes. To collect a lot of knowledge so as to become a well-informed citizen? Yes. But there is far more that he should expect: namely to give and to get in a community of minds and personalities. In this community of minds and personalities a number of things need to be happening, and happening all together. The man will be learning about his own subjects in more depth. He will also be discovering what other people's subjects are about, his mental curiosity being stretched and his imagination widened. This widening happens partly through the element of breadth in certain parts of the curriculum and partly through the large unofficial world of intellectual activities which surround the working hours. The man too will expect teachers of more than one sort. Some will be teachers with a gift for being interested not only in their subject but in people, and they can help the student to find himself mentally and spiritually. Other teachers, without necessarily being less human, will be devoting themselves to research and the enlargement of knowledge; and I would say that a university fails unless every undergraduate absorbs a little of the inspiration from being in a place where there are people devoted to the pursuit of the sciences and the arts for their own sake. All these things mixed together make up the virtue of a good university. The community aspect of it is vital. It means that minds are trained in such a way that character is inevitably being trained as well. It is not difficult to produce sophisticated men and women by collecting them to learn certain subjects. But it is not sophisticated men and women that a good university tries to produce. It is men and women whose knowledge goes with character, and with reverence for persons and for the things of the mind.

So, my Lords, when we talk about the quality of standards it is something like *that* which we mean. And when we ask whether these standards will continue amid a vast expansion we have to realize that already they are greatly under strain. At present there are too many university students who have a lonely life in lodgings, long distances to travel daily, and little of the intellectual community which is so important. At present there are too many courses which lack the proper personal relation of teachers and students. It is also alarming to know that already, in the years 1959–61, only 52% of the intake of new university teachers had themselves first-class degrees. Already there come to our universities some entrants with little ability to give and to get in the way that a university needs. This has nothing to do with social background or the wage-group of their parents—nothing whatever. It is to do with a failure to have the mind able to take its part in the institution for their mutual good.

Here, my Lords, I would say something about selection. The problem of selection has not really been solved either by the universities or by the schools or by the Robbins Report. The Robbins Report approaches the question most helpfully, but I wish it had probed into it further. The only method so far discovered is to pick boys and girls who secure the highest marks in the appointed test. But I am sure it is possible for a boy (or girl) to obtain a high mark at that stage and yet to have exhausted his mental powers and mental ambitions in the process. He has gone mentally as far as he will go at that stage, and does not enter into what is going to be offered to him in the university. It is possible too for a pupil at school to be less able to hit a high notch in university entrance, and yet to be capable of all the development which university life calls for. The Robbins Committee mentions the need to look at the pupil's school record over back years. But do we not need more than that, if only we could discover *what*.

The Americans use the word "motivation", and so does the Robbins Report, without pursuing the matter far. "Why do you want to go to the university? What do you hope to do, to learn, to become, when you get there?" That is what we want to discover about the aspirant to a university place.

This means, my Lords, that on any showing the problem of selection cannot be solved by seeing school and university as separate worlds. Other things too point to the interrelation of school problems and university problems, including the relation between broad courses and specialized courses. The university problems partly begin in the sixth form and indeed in the fifth form at school. For that reason I support the plea made by my old friend Mr Shearman in his dissentient note in the Report that it would be a pity to have two ministries dealing with education rather than one. I think his plea has great force.

My Lords, it has been said that the Robbins Report forecasts a revolution in our national life. So it does, and I believe it is a revolution that is overdue. I have put to your Lordships some considerations about the question whether standards will be maintained. And my plea is that the quality of these standards is bound up not just with certain factors being numerically maintained but with the holding of these factors together in intellectual communities with a certain kind of ideal at work in them.

If standards are to be maintained and to grow there must be no diminution for reasons of economy of the caveats which the Robbins Report makes, and we need to be looking at the secret of quality more closely even than the Robbins Report does.

Within this coming era of expansion the Church in which I hold office, and I am sure all the Churches, will give to the schools and universities the utmost service which they can. Left to itself expansion can extend the weaknesses as well as the virtues of our present university life. We do not as a country want sophisticated men and women. We want men and women whose acquisition of knowledge has come together with growth in character, with humility before life's mysteries, and with reverence, reverence for persons and reverence for the things of the mind.

In Memory of
President Kennedy

A faithful Creator.
1 Pet. 4.19

I speak to each one of you who is sharing in this service, here in St Paul's, or in your home in this country, or in America, or anywhere in the world. Your heart at this time is in its sorrow nearer to the hearts of thousands all over the world than it can have been for a very long time. Why is this? It is because President Kennedy was one who touched something universal in the human heart. Thinking of him we all see so vividly what we admire in a human life, and what are the great causes we care about. The man: brave to the point of heroism as his actions in wartime showed, youthful beyond the age when youthfulness always lasts, tenacious when there could be no compromise, infinitely patient when the human touch could win conciliation, and all the time with a lovely home and family around him. There was the man. And the causes—how they too touch the mind and conscience as well as the heart—peace, freedom, the service of prosperous nations to nations where there is poverty and hunger, the partnership of every race in civil rights.

There was the man, and there the causes; and in a moment of madness the man was done to death, and the causes lose a champion just coming to the prime of his powers. To what purpose is this waste? Men of faith, of every faith and of none, find that question piercing them like a knife.

"A faithful Creator." Here in God's presence we Christian people stammer out those words, "a faithful Creator", "a faithful Creator". We repeat the words not as hiding like ostriches from the sight of evil and sorrow. No, rather seeing evil and sorrow fully in the face we believe that a good Creator holds our little world in his hands, hands of infinite love and power. Evil there is, and evil destroys and divides; call it crime or call it madness, it does its worst. But without turning away from evil we see beyond it God's own answer to it in the Cross of Christ on Calvary and the Resurrection on Easter morning—for there it is apparent how God can turn suffering into a triumph of love and sacrifice, and how God shows the gate to an everlasting life before which the life we know is but a little prelude. Such is our Christian faith. It is a faith costly and glorious—costly, for it is no escapism, no hiding from facts, with sacrifice at its heart—glorious, because it sees man's destiny reaching beyond the miseries of the moment. And in the light of Calvary and Easter just when our faith seemed to be shattered we found the words returning "a faithful Creator". Yes, "a faithful Creator".

What then follows, for President Kennedy, for the world, for us? He is now committed into his own Creator's hands; surrounded and followed by the prayers of so many; no end, but rather a beginning as he goes nearer to the love, the wisdom, the beauty of the God he has always worshipped. "Let light perpetual shine upon him." And here on earth his service to the world, to humanity is not ended. The shock of his loss brings home to you his example, his ideals, his character; in our loss we realize him with a new vividness, and this more vivid impact of him after tragedy is very real. The impact of his example will help and inspire men and women for time yet to come. So too the causes which he cared for so greatly will be served, must be served with new determination. Peace was one. Freedom was another. Yet another was the cause of hungry peoples, a cause for which he pleaded not just because it was expedient but because it was right. And so too the cause of racial brotherhood. His leadership is no more. His example stays for us to follow.

"A faithful Creator." In his good and loving hands is the man whom we mourn to-day. In his hands too is the world we live in, the causes we must serve. But it is in the heart and the conscience

of each man and woman that the issue lies. For a faithful Creator
made not just the world in a lump but every one of us his human
creatures, each of us with a mind to know him, a heart to love
him, a will to serve him. "I come from God, I belong to God, I
go to God"; that is the reason, the meaning of each of us. There
is an old English prayer the words of which tell of what a Christian will at this moment want to say, and as I read it you will find
it to be your own.

> Thanks be to thee, O Lord Jesus Christ,
> for all the benefits thou hast won for me,
> for all the pains and insults thou hast borne for me.
> O most merciful redeemer, friend, and brother,
> may I know thee more clearly,
> love thee more dearly,
> and follow thee more nearly.

BIOGRAPHY

Charles Simeon:
Evangelical and Churchman

The second centenary of the birth of Charles Simeon recalls one who was both a great Evangelical and a great Churchman. It is hard to imagine him anywhere else but in the Church of England, and he is one of those figures who help to explain the Church of England to itself in any age.

Simeon endured much within the Church he loved so well. In November 1792 there were astonishing sights at Holy Trinity, Cambridge. A congregation so resentful of the new evangelical vicar that the pew-holders absented themselves to a man, locking their high enclosed pews so that no one else could get into them. The people who cared to come, sitting on benches put by the vicar in the aisles. The churchwardens removing the benches with their own hands. The afternoon service in the hands of a lecturer preaching "against" the vicar. The vicar trying to retrieve the situation by holding an evening service, but finding the church locked and the churchwarden keeping the key in his pocket. It was indeed a critical question, What could be the relation between evangelical revival and the ordered life of the historic Church?

When men preach Christ as dying men to dying men, the urgency is overwhelming. If the walls of your own parish church exclude you, preach Christ in houses, barns, coalmines, anywhere. If you find a parish in which there are starving souls, why wait for the permission of a vicar, or the authority of a bishop? So Berridge of Everton, preaching from parish to parish, said, "Must salvation give place to a faithful decency? Must sinners go flocking to hell through our dread of irregularity? If they have tasted of manna, they cannot feed on legal crusts, though baked by some staunch pharisee right up to perfection." But the danger is plain. Souls are saved into sects here and sects there, conscious of being the true Church of the converted—a perilous thing to be, because it, in its turn, can be "baked" by its own "staunch pharisees" into a self-conscious perfectionism.

Such was the problem. Was evangelical revival to find its home within the Church of England, not substituting a "faithful decency" for salvation, but using the "faithful decency" of Anglican ways in the service of salvation? It was Charles Simeon who was himself the answer.

How was he converted? As a freshman at King's, he was in touch with no evangelical group or evangelical leaders. But he was required, as a member of the college, to receive the Holy Sacrament. How could he? How dare he? How could sinful man come so near to his Lord? For three weeks he prayed, he read, he fasted; tears often flowed; he became prostrate with illness. But he came to realize that the Lord who was coming to feed his soul was the same Lord who had borne his sins on Calvary. That was the answer—the crucified sin-bearer and the Holy Sacrament. It was in the heart of the Church, amid the "faithful decency" of its central rite, that Simeon found Christ, and peace.

What then became Simeon's attitude to the Church of England? He endured more within her than without her. But he found her true meaning, beneath all the failings of her contemporary members, in the Book of Common Prayer. "The Bible first, and the Prayer Book next; and all other books and doings in subordination to both." That was the order. He loved the Prayer Book, because the Prayer Book brings the Bible to us, not just according to our fancy or choice or taste or impulse, but in the ordered wisdom of the ordered family life of the Church, with the round of festival and fast, of lection and psalm, of rites and services touching every crisis in human life from birth to death. Simeon preached before the University a course of sermons on "The Excellency of the Liturgy". He said, "The finest sight short of heaven would be a whole congregation using the prayers of the liturgy in the true spirit of them". He felt that "the written prayers meet all that a sinner needs". He was never harsh towards

Dissenters. "I dare not blame a man for going where he thinks that his soul can be fed. . . . But, be cautious of separation."

From the firm Prayer Book churchmanship of Charles Simeon, there sprang two great results, the one for this country and the other for the Church beyond the seas.

Here at home Simeon's influence linked the evangelical revival within the Church of England decisively with the parochial system. Simeon lived out himself, and encouraged in others, the ideal of the parochial pastor. The pastor, he says, "has more to do in the study and in the closet than even in the cottage". That is a strong statement of how the parish parson's mission to souls goes with his prayer and his study. He works within his own allotted sphere as a man under authority with his soldiers under him—the laymen whom he trains like elders to be his fellow-workers in the care of the parish. The parochial system is still the pattern of the life of our Church in England. To Simeon we owe it that the evangelical spirit has moved within it, and not apart from it. Before he died, Simeon had created a trust which purchased the patronage of benefices so as to secure continuity of evangelical teaching in them. I do not now speak about the evils to which trust patronage can lead; I note only that the original aim and the original result was to strengthen the parochial system by bringing within it an apostolic zeal which might otherwise have been apart from it.

It was in relation to the Church overseas that the other still more decisive result of Simeon's influence took place. The missionary impulse was growing. S.P.G. had started in 1701, S.P.C.K. in 1698. But what form would the missionary impulse springing from the evangelical revival finally take? In 1795 the undenominational London Missionary Society was formed; churchmen and dissenters were both in it; it sprang from that impulse to win souls for Christ which asks few questions about Church and order and discipline. It was to be a society with a great history; David Livingstone was to go under its aegis to Africa. But it came in the end to have no link with the life of the Church of England. It might have been that the whole evangelical missionary enterprise had run on in that way. But not so Charles Simeon. He persuaded a conference of his friends that the new undenominational society was "not formed upon those principles which justify our publicly uniting with them". So there came about from 1799 the Church Missionary Society. It was a decisive event for the ultimate future of what was to become the Anglican Communion throughout the world. Just as at home Simeon's influence caused evangelical zeal to flow into the ordered life and steady discipline of the parochial system, so overseas it caused the same zeal for the winning of souls to flow into the building up on every continent of that ordered portion of the Holy Catholic Church which we now call the Anglican Communion.

What is the Anglican Communion to-day? It is the creation of the blending of ardent missionary zeal and the ordered life of the Church based upon the Prayer Book. It is a group of Churches describable in Simeon's words as standing up "the Bible first, the Prayer Book next"; and to possess the Prayer Book is to possess, along with the Bible, the creeds, the sacraments, the threefold ministry of bishops, priests, and deacons, handed down from the apostles' time. To-day the Anglican Communion embraces people of every continent, of many races, of many political allegiances, outside as well as inside the British Commonwealth; and it embraces them within a Church life based upon no more and no less than those principles upon which Christendom may one day unite—catholic, evangelical, scriptural. The place of Charles Simeon in the making of the Anglican Communion is one which it is hard to exaggerate.

Churchmanship and evangelicalism properly belong together, and for Charles Simeon they were inseparable. They went apart subsequently when, in fear of the churchmanship of Tractarians and Ritualists, the Evangelicals entangled themselves in a "low-churchery" foreign to their tradition. To-day we are learning within the Church of England a greater brotherhood, "high and low, rich and poor, one with another". There is on all sides a readiness to see how closely word and sacrament, scripture and liturgy, go together; and their unity was never taught more clearly than by Simeon. But he warns us against mere "moderation". He once said, playfully, "Truth is not in the middle, and not in one extreme, but in both extremes. So that if extremes please you, I am your man; only remember that it is not one extreme we are to go to, but both extremes." Half playful, half serious, these words have much to say to us. Simeon himself went to extremes in two ways: in devotion to the Church, and in abasement before his Crucified Saviour.

Dean Church
and the
Growth of Anglicanism

The new biography of Dean Church confers upon its readers the threefold benefit of a first-rate book to enjoy, a vivid picture of one of the greatest of Anglicans, and some help in seeing some of our present problems of Church and religion in the perspective of history. That is the tribute of gratitude which I would pay to B. A. Smith and the Oxford Press for *Dean Church, the Anglican Response to Newman*.

When the veterans of the Oxford Movement turned to Dean Church for the writing of its history, they looked to one who, for all the detached wisdom which was his greatest quality, had been through the conflict with the glint of battle in his eye. It is indeed true that "in the thick of an honest mêlée, Church was the partisan *par excellence*. He perhaps more than any other of the Tractarians appreciated the movement as a movement in the clannish sense." And he was devoted to Newman. Is not Newman's influence discernible in Church's style? I have sometimes felt that Church's prose at its best is nearer to Newman than any other prose of the century—in rhythm, in simplicity, and in the conveying of "something unearthly" to the reader. No one could have felt the shock of Newman's secession in 1846 more keenly than the writer of the most poignant of all descriptions of it: "We sat glumly at our breakfasts every morning, and then someone came in with news of something disagreeable—someone gone, someone sure to go."

Of the men who stayed to vindicate the catholicity of the Church of England, Pusey and Keble represented the unbending orthodoxy of the first Tractarians; James Mozley had the acutest theological mind—with a readiness for independence; and R. W. Church was strong in respect of two things where the rest were weak—the cool judgement brought by a sense of history, and the conviction that civilization and culture (even when contaminated by paganism) have a positive meaning for the Christian. In both respects the disciple had what the master had lacked. Contrast Newman, thrown off his balance by contemporary ecclesiastical troubles, and Church undismayed (however pained) by a Gorham judgement. Contrast the foreign travel of the two men: Newman shrinking from the sights of paganism as the symbols of the foes of faith, Church rejoicing in art and culture, Italian, Greek, and Moslem.

In 1853 Church, now 38 years old and recently married, left Oxford for the Somersetshire living of Whatley. There he spent eighteen years as a country rector until his acceptance in 1871, with the utmost reluctance, of the Deanery of St Paul's. Throughout the years his influence grew, though his writings were seldom other than "occasional", and his share in official business was small. It was the influence of a temper of mind which he brought to bear upon movements, policies, and personalities; and that temper of mind was his finest gift to his times and legacy to the years which followed. At St Paul's he was at the head of one of the great Cathedral Chapters of all time—Lightfoot, Liddon, Stubbs, Holland, and Gregory; and by his friendship with Gladstone he influenced the Prime Minister's appointments. But the attachment to Gladstone, like the attachment to Newman, led to pain and disillusion; for after many years in which Church and Gladstone had shared a growing liberality in matters of Church and State, Church found the policies of Gladstone's old age wrongheaded and unconvincing, and "for the second time in my life I have to try as well as I can to unite unabated admiration with the impossibility of moral or intellectual agreement".

Through and after the days of shock and secession, Church was utterly convinced of the Anglican position. But it was the conviction of a quiet and sober faith, without glow or bombast. He wrote of "a new school whose main purpose was to see things as

they are: which had learned by experience to distrust unqualified
admiration and unqualified disparagements, determined not to be
blinded even by genius to plain certainties". Church saw in the
Oxford Movement the gateway to a view of the Anglican vocation
larger and less cramped than the interpretations which had pre-
viously prevailed. The classic statement of his view is the essay
on Lancelot Andrewes in the volume *Pascal and other sermons*.
Here Church insists that the English Reformation was not completed in the reign of Elizabeth, but includes what happened down
to 1662 and the later Carolines. The reconstruction of the Church
(which was essentially the same Church as before) was a vast
undertaking, for which the knowledge, wisdom, and balance of
view were not all accessible in the first stage. Much in the first
stage was hasty and provisional, and the last word was not spoken
by Cranmer, Hooper, and Jewel. There was a century of adjust-
ment by divines who worked out the appeal to antiquity with a
fullness and balance not always attained by the divines who first
proclaimed the necessity of that appeal.

Church believed that in his own day this larger view of Anglicanism was being jeopardized by attempts to force upon the
Church an unduly narrow view of its doctrine and vocation.
Hence his strong criticism of the authority of the Judicial Committee of the Privy Council, and of the attempts to suppress not
only vestments but even the "eastward position" as well. He insisted that Parliamentary control of the Church was not a necessary corollary of the Royal Supremacy, and that "Court-made
doctrine" was a violation of the Church's proper liberty; and,
though himself no Ritualist, he resisted the pressure to which the
Ritualists were being subjected. Yet because to him catholicity and
liberality went closely together, he shrank from a hostile attitude
to *any* minority group or tendency. While others denounced Sir
John Seeley's *Ecce Homo* for its failure to assert the Deity of
Christ, Church welcomed it for what it was—the sincere testimony
of an historian to the uniqueness of Christ's humanity.

Next to the new light which he throws upon Church's relation
with many contemporary personalities, there is the great value of

B. A. Smith's account of Church's writings and thought. Church was above all else both a great teacher of religion and a great student of humanity, and he was nowhere more at home than in seeing some clash of personalities, or some tragic epoch, or some phase of civilization against the background of those truths of religion which he could specially bring home: the Cross as the measure of success or failure, the reality of God's providential government, the constant nearness of another world. These characteristics are present alike in the studies of Anselm and Dante, in the history of the Oxford Movement, in the *Gifts of Civilization*, and in some of the sermons scattered in other volumes. Amongst the latter, some seem to me to equal any teaching of the simple profundities of religion which exist in our language: "Failures in Life", "The Imperfections of Religious Men", "Human Life in the light of Immortality", "A Particular Providence", "The Times and Seasons of God's Working"; and with Church, as with Newman, to those who know just a little of the writer the titles themselves have their own revealing eloquence.

To read the new biography of Dean Church and to renew in consequence the friendship of some of his writings, is to have some searchings of heart about the present. How great is the need of Church's vigour of mind, and sensitivity to movements of thought without as well as within the Christian community. But perhaps the biggest need is not the analysis of problems and of the applications of religion to them—but really great teaching about religion itself, which would have its own light to throw.

Herbert Hensley Henson

The love of Christ constraineth us.
2 Cor. 5.14

Let it be my privilege to recall to you to-day one of the most
eminent of Fellows of All Souls, the centenary of whose birth
falls in the present year : Herbert Hensley Henson. History knows
him as one of the great bishops of Durham, but it was All Souls
which gave him his first deep happiness, evoked his lifelong
affection, and fortified him more than once in times of trial.

A lover of books from early childhood, Henson often grieved
that he had no proper schooling; the home was at Broadstairs,
where the father and mother lived with their seven children. They
were "comfortably off", but the father became indifferent to the
children's education through his narrow evangelical piety which
became morbid and fanatical after his wife's death, when Herbert
was six. A little later the father married again and Herbert's stepmother encouraged his love for reading; and "it was to my
stepmother I owe it that I was sent to Oxford. With difficulty she
persuaded my father to consent, but only on condition that my
expenditure was as small as possible, and my academic career was
as brief as was consistent with my taking a degree".[1] There followed three rather lonely years as a non-collegiate student. Then
came a first in Modern History, and a fellowship at All Souls.

I was not quite twenty-one when I became a Fellow of All
Souls, still young enough to form friendships and to dream
dreams. The society into which I found myself so unexpectedly
introduced gave me just what I wanted, a larger outlook, contact with intellectual superiors, an atmosphere of vivid and

[1] *Retrospect of an Unimportant Life*, vol. 1, p. 4.

varied culture. There was nothing in my previous life to prepare me for the new experience, nothing to hinder me in yielding freely to its influence. I loved everybody from the warden to the scout's boy, and now after more than half a century I never enter the college without emotion.[2]

Looking ahead it is interesting to notice that when in 1913 Henson left Westminster for the Deanery of Durham his friends in the Convocation of Canterbury gave him a parting gift; it was a beautiful copy of Vallance's *The Old Colleges of Oxford* which they gave him, and they inscribed it to him as "Veritatis, justitiae, liberalitatis, eloquenti et strenuo propugnatori". Those were the qualities which All Souls saw in him, the qualities which through many years he brought to bear upon Church and nation.

Ordination was for Henson the result of deep conviction. Self-conscious, sensitive, combative in temperament, he was moved by a sense of dedication to a divine Lord, his piety being derived from his home and modified by the tensions of culture and criticism. Ordained by Bishop Stubbs at Cuddesdon on the "title" of his fellowship, Henson went away very soon, first to the Oxford House in Bethnal Green and from there to the charge of the great industrial parish of Barking at the youthful age of twenty-five. Barking saw a side of Henson of which All Souls could only have had glimpses, a love of people of every kind and a courage in opposing popular causes. At a time when Trades Unionism was growing in power in the locality, Henson preached some courageous sermons at crowded services for working-men, criticizing some of the current "labour" assumptions and pleading that temperance, purity, charity, and personal repentance before Christ crucified were worth more than political action. It was ever typical of Henson to be critical of "Causes" on behalf of humanity in the lump, and to care greatly for the individual man and woman. What Barking was to mean to him through the years is seen in some words of one of his episcopal charges long years after:

[2] *Op. cit.*, p. 5.

The happiest years of my ministry were those in which as the vicar of a great industrial parish I was nearest to the people. Faces look out from the past, toil-worn faces radiant with love and confidence. Nothing of what men call success is worth comparing with the experiences which those faces recall. ... I say to you then, love God and love your people. Count nothing excessive which you can do for them. Serve them in your office for the love of Christ, and they will give you back more than you can give them.[3]

Five years in Barking were a severe tax on Henson's health and nerve. He welcomed appointment to the non-parochial church of St Mary's Hospital, Ilford, where despite continuous preaching he found leisure for reading and his appetite for public controversy. To this period belongs his open letter to Lord Halifax on the ritual controversy entitled *Cui Bono?*, the first of a long series of brilliant polemical pieces. In the first year of the new century Henson's great opportunity came. The invitation from Lord Salisbury to a Canonry at Westminster with the Rectory of St Margaret's gave him the scene of a ministry at Westminster for twelve years. It was a preaching ministry of power and influence. Always in his own pulpit and giving as much care to his weekly sermons as scholars give to their books, Henson helped many people who were feeling their way towards an intelligent faith. His prose was a little rhetorical, but clear and lucid. His themes were the central ones of the New Testament. His attitude was liberal, but less typical of contemporary modernism than of (in his own words) "a latitude man who had strayed from the seventeenth century into the twentieth". If the most sensational episode in his preaching was his denunciation of the atrocities of the Peruvian–Amazon Company on the Putamayo, his characteristic contemporary concerns were to plead for fraternity with the nonconformists and all the Reformed Churches, to uphold the establishment of the Church against those high-churchmen who were eager to sever the Church and State connection, and to pro-

[3] *Ad Clerum*, p. 210.

tect critical scholars in freedom for their studies. The last matter saw Henson in eager controversy. To him the Incarnation was a supernatural fact, and Christ was indubitably divine; but he was concerned to protect within the Church and its ministry those who were, on historical grounds, hesitant about the particular mode of the Birth and the Resurrection of the Saviour. However, to read Henson's Westminster sermons now is to be more aware of the vigorous and positive exposition of the Apostolic Creed than of the particular points which came to be seized upon as heterodox.

It was in Henson's Westminster years that the duel began between him and Charles Gore, at first a fellow Canon but leaving in 1902 to be Bishop in turn of Worcester, Birmingham, and Oxford. They were friends, both were powerful preachers and men of moral leadership; but how different! Gore, aristocratic by birth, Catholic, theologically minded, socialistic: Henson, a *novus homo*, liberal, historically minded, individualistic. Each man became the foil of the other; their differences, their battles, their friendship, their comprehension within our Church itself tells the story and describes the genius of Anglicanism in this century.

From 1913 to 1917, Henson was Dean of Durham. It was his first taste of the north he was to love so well. Then, near the end of 1917, there came "the Hereford Scandal". It was Lloyd George's first episcopal nomination; it was not desired by Archbishop Davidson, who valued Henson's talents but would have preferred to see him chosen a little later for some industrial see. It led to a storm about Henson's alleged heterodoxy. There were some like Gore who were troubled about the proper limits of interpretation of the historical clauses in the Creed. There were others who pursued an unscrupulous heresy hunt, publishing *catenae* of quotations out of their context. I would to-day dwell not on the painful episode, but on the outcome. Henson went to his consecration on 2 February 1819 with harassed mind and wounded heart; the friendship of All Souls never meant more to him than now. Subsequently, Henson for a time put aside controversy and gave himself for two years to the care of the Herefordshire parishes, delighting in his visits and confirmations and proving himself friend and father in the simplicity of Christ's service. This was the part of his character about which many people did not know, and which his public life sometimes did much to conceal. But no record of Henson is true which does not remember it. There is the power of the heart to heal and to steady the conflicts of the mind.

In 1920, Henson, again on Lloyd George's invitation, betook himself to Durham and to the Palatine see. Here he was to delight in the associations of history which belong to Durham perhaps more than to any other see in the country, and in his home at Auckland Castle where so much of that history is represented. Here is the banqueting-hall of Bishop Pudsey beautifully transformed by Bishop Cosin into the chapel, where are the graves of Cosin, Lightfoot, and Westcott. Here too is the wing built by Tunstall, and the path along which Butler used to walk as he meditated. Fortified by an historical setting which means much to every bishop of Durham, Henson was a very conscientious diocesan; and it is a strenuous life with many parochial visits and confirmations in the coldest months of a severe climate. The diocese was somewhat in awe of him, but came through the years to love him. His biting satire could not long conceal a very kind and generous heart, and to answer him back was sometimes the way to trust and friendship. Meanwhile the Church in general and the country knew him chiefly from controversy, oratory, and epigrams, and there were two changes, one of them apparent and the other real and deliberate, in his ecclesiastical position.

First, it seemed to a good many people that Henson moved away from the "modernism" which he had expounded in the Westminster years. The Diary of Dean Inge contains some caustic references to Henson as a sort of lost leader of liberalism. Thus, Inge and his wife are Henson's guests at Auckland in September 1921, and Inge writes:

At Auckland Castle, a very grand house. I had a not very satisfactory talk with Herbert. He is unstable as water. Liberalism in theology will not get much more help from Herbert Dunelm.

Kitty (Mrs Inge) judged rather differently. "There is a serious-ness and a wisdom about his outlook on the world which I have not noticed before. I feel now that he will be quite the best to succeed Cantuar, and sit in St Augustine's Chair."

I would myself put the matter thus. Henson had never been a deep theologian. As an historian he had been concerned to protect for himself and for others the rights of the scholar's integrity in historical criticism, but he was at heart a believer in a Divine Saviour and not interested in the philosophic aspects of modern-ism. Now, he came to feel that contemporary modernism, as seen in some of the papers at the Modern Churchmen's Conference at Girton in 1921, had come to mean not simply the rights of his-torical criticism but an *a priori* philosophy which obscured the dis-tinction of Godhead and manhood and adopted an attitude of academic patronage instead of adoring homage towards the person of Christ. From this Henson recoiled; at heart he was before all else the worshipper of a Divine Saviour, and his heart won.

Tell them [he writes in a letter [4] to Alfred Fawkes] to remem-ber that Christianity is Christ's religion, and cannot survive any handling of the Founder which removes Him from the kind of supremacy He has ever held. No version of Christian theology which does not preserve the proportion and essential content of apostolic Christianity as disclosed in the New Testament can serve the turn of the modern Church. Foakes-Jackson and Kirsop Lake have drifted into a position towards Christ which no convert in any age could adopt: it is external, patronizing, profane. People feel this: and only feel it the more since they cannot see always how to justify the feeling.

The real alteration in Henson's belief was that which concerned the Establishment of the Church of England. He took a notable part in the controversy about the revision of the Prayer Book which was rejected by the House of Commons in 1927, castigating the opponents of the revision as "the Protestant underworld", an

4 Quoted in A. M. Ramsey, *From Gore to Temple*, p. 87.

army of "illiterates generalled by octogenarians" and comparing one of the prelates who led the opposition to St Simon Stylites as "he combines the remoteness of the saint with the rigidity of the pillar". After the vote of the House of Commons shortly before Christmas 1927, Henson burnt his ships and came out as a determined advocate of disestablishment, declaring his faith in a sermon before the University of Cambridge on the text "Shall two walk together except they be agreed?". The decision appeared to be sudden, and it did not lack its dramatic and oratorical possibilities. But as time passed and Henson's mind disclosed itself, especially in his book *Disestablishment* (1932), it was apparent that the change had been growing in his mind for some while, perhaps half-consciously, and that it rested not only upon the fate of the Revised Prayer Book but upon a sense that the growing secularism of English life was making establishment an anachronism. Thereafter, standing to his new guns, Henson refused to touch any of the proposals for patching or modifying the establishment which subsequently came to the fore.

Within his own diocese, there were the terrible years of industrial depression. First the conflict in the coalfields and later the unemployment in the shipyards. Moved to the heart by these tragedies, Henson was none the less led by integrity of conscience and judgement to refuse assent to the socialist ideas of the labour community in County Durham. Where his penultimate predecessor Westcott had been, broadly, socialistic and with the tide, Henson must needs be individualistic and against the tide. It cost him popularity, it made enemies for him, but it did not reduce his efforts to help in the relief of distress and it drew out his personal courage. Driving into a hostile crowd of miners at Ferryhill, he stepped out of the car and addressed the crowd, telling them about his experiences in Barking, of the sufferings caused by dear coal, and of what cheaper coal could do for the country and consequently for the miners themseves. They listened, they respected, they cheered.

For eighteen years the Durham episcopate ran on. Henson felt increasingly the dark shadows across the country and the world, the growing secularism and the economic frustrations at home and abroad, the persecutions of the Jews and the invasion of Abyssinia, which moved him to the depths. His diary discloses his wistful self-consciousness about himself and his career (with a half-wish to become Archbishop of York when Lang was translated to succeed Davidson in 1928), his sensitiveness, his frequent epigrams. But these characteristics were met within him by his affectionate heart and his will to see himself humbled before the Crucified; "There is nothing like the Psalms to set one right", he wrote once on turning to the Psalter on a day of strains. His friend and foil, Charles Gore, used to speak of the Christian attitude as one of proximate pessimism and ultimate faith. Such increasingly was Henson's mood; it was apparent in his choice of favoured texts for his sermons: "Jesus Christ the same yesterday, to-day, and for ever", "I see that all things come to an end, but Thy commandment is exceedingly broad", "He endured, as seeing Him who is invisible".

Henson found himself increasingly isolated from the prevailing movements and enthusiasms in the Church in the years between the wars. He felt that the Anglo-Catholics were distorting the historic meaning of Anglicanism (though he eventually found himself nearer to them on the issue of the liberty of the Church). He alienated the Evangelicals by his trenchant attacks on their patronage trusts. He abhorred Oxford Groupism. He criticized "the sentimental socialistic version of Christianity which has its Nicaea in Copec and its Mecca at Bishopthorpe". Yet by his integrity, his grasp of an older tradition of Anglicanism represented by some of his great predecessors in the see of Durham, and his belief in straightforward pastoral duty as the key to the Church's life, his influence not indeed upon the policies and administration of the Church but upon the clergy and laity was deeper and wider than was easily apparent. His influence has persisted. To-day, when his controversial writings are seldom read and his Gifford lectures on *Christian Morality* are forgotten, his books of pastoral counsel, *Church and Parson in England*, 1927, and *Ad Clerum*, 1935, are read and remembered.

Let Henson, however, sum up his own episcopate. The occasion is the presentation to him of his portrait in Auckland Castle.

From the pictures which hang on these walls I will select five; Tunstall, Morton, Cosin, Butler, Van Mildert. These bishops reigned in evil times, and their names carry suggestions of conflict and controversy. Tunstall had to live through the critical years which witnessed the Reformation and died, a very old man, a prisoner of state. Morton had to sustain the terrific shock of the Puritan revolution, and in his extreme old age died in poverty. Cosin, after traversing land and sea as an exile during the great Rebellion, carried through the restoration of the Church in Durham. Butler had another kind of conflict to wage. He upheld the standard of the faith against deism and erastianism. Van Mildert witnessed the passing away of the Palatine dignity which for so many centuries had adorned the mitre of Durham; he lived through the first tempestuous phase of modern democracy. In future years, when I too have become a memory and a symbol, I wonder whether my name will also be associated with crisis and calamity. One thing is certain, and illustrated by the long history which the series of the Bishops represents, that in the great Huguenot's words "the Church of God is an anvil which has broken many hammers".

When in November 1920 I was enthroned as Bishop of Durham . . . I remember naming Morton as the Bishop whose character and fortune appealed to me most strongly, and I read out the contemporary description of him that he was "small in stature, upright in person, sprightly in motion, and preserved the vigour of youth in extreme old age". Bishop Morton lived to be 95. It is related of him that when by the triumphant Puritans he was driven from his bishopric and reduced to actual poverty he fell in with a Puritan acquaintance who, affecting not to recognize him, inquired who he was. "I am that old man, the Bishop of Durham", was the answer, "in spite of all your votes." . . . We need not doubt it. God is with us as He was with our fathers.[5]

[5] *The Bishoprick*, February 1930, vol. vi, no. 2.

A few months before the beginning of the Hitler war, Henson retired to live in Suffolk. He planned to read and write, and he tells of how he put on one side of his study the volumes of the Dictionary of National Biography, the Loeb classics, and the Cambridge syndicated histories, and above them a beautiful crucifix brought home from the continent, to represent how our European civilization stands under the judgement of the Crucified. His retirement was interrupted when in 1940 Mr Churchill recalled him to a canonry at Westminster, certain that this brave old bishop and patriot would be able to hearten the people from the pulpit he had known many years before. So it was, with the bombs falling around; but only for a few months. Failing eyesight made it impossible for Henson to carry out his canonical duties, and he resigned. The last years were spent in Suffolk, and the aged Bishop preached sermons to the village congregation, unable to read a manuscript in the pulpit and compelled to give *ex tempore* discourses such as he had always eschewed. He could, however, complete the three volumes of his *Retrospect of an Unimportant Life*. He saw the end of the war. He died on 27 September 1947.

There was in Henson's career one most interesting "might-have-been", when in the middle of the Westminster years Asquith invited him to come to Oxford as Professor of Ecclesiastical History. "The waters are somewhat stagnant," wrote Asquith, "and it is time that they should be moved." It was a hard decision, because Henson loved Oxford and loved history. The decision was the very conscientious one that after some years away from academic discipline he could only hope as Professor for "the kind and measure of success which Stanley obtained", i.e. the literary and picturesque exposition of history, and that this would fall below his own scholarly conscience. With some pangs, but with conviction, the choice was made. Perhaps the truth is that Henson lacked one of the scholar's qualities, patience. When in his writings he takes his readers most fascinatingly into an historical theme and the reader would like to linger there, Henson all too quickly returns to the pointing of contemporary morals. Well it was that there was in store for him not a life in Oxford but the great years in Durham.

If it was Cambridge that gave to Durham both Lightfoot and Westcott, no less is it true that All Souls gave Henson. It was here that he *found himself*, warm in heart and eager in mind, *justitiae, veritatis, liberalitatis propugnator*. But no merely human phenomena suffice to explain his life, with a unity amid its many contradictions and a constant humbling of nature's capacities beneath something greater than themselves. *Caritas Christi urget nos*. That was the inner meaning. And "the love of Christ constraineth us, because we thus judge that one died for all, therefore all died; and he died for all that they which live should no longer live unto themselves but unto him who for their sakes died and rose again . . . old things are passed away; behold they are become new". To this faith Herbert Hensley Henson dedicated himself, and by this faith alone he would now be judged.

Lionel Thornton: Theologian

My friendship with Lionel Thornton began when I was an undergraduate in the nineteen-twenties and he was spending some months in Cambridge at the Oratory House on a kind of sabbatical leave from his lectures and teaching at Mirfield. He was a lively talker, and always talked theology with a lucidity which his writings sometimes lacked. His talk made me conscious that he stood in a great tradition of Anglican divinity: the tradition embodied in some of his seniors in the Community of the Resurrection, Frere, Figgis, Edward Talbot. It was a tradition at once ascetical and incarnational, catholic and liberal. Thornton had already borne witness to this tradition in his first book, *Conduct and the Supernatural* (1917), and in his book on *Richard Hooker* (1923). It was about the time when I first knew him that he was moving to the front rank of contemporary theologians in the essay on "The Doctrine of God" in *Essays Catholic and Critical* (1926), and in *The Incarnate Lord* (1928).

The book on Hooker is now, alas, forgotten. But it deserves to be recalled as a superb piece of Anglican interpretation, and as a clue to the growth of Thornton's own thinking. He saw Hooker as marking the divide between Anglican theology and some of the trends of Reformed theology. The putting of the appeal to reason next to the appeal to scripture, the recovery of the doctrine of creation through the use of the concept of the "laws", and above all the relating of the Sacraments directly to the Word Incarnate and not only to the Word Spoken, were all of the utmost significance. In much Reformation theology "a closed circle was drawn round the inward personal element in religion; and the world of external things became sharply separated from the world of interior personal experience. Thus the 'thing-element' in our world lost much of its religious significance".[1] Though Hooker did not wholly avoid this error, he led the way from it, and Anglican incarnational and sacramental theology could build on his foundations. Thornton shows how these issues reappear in modern times in the contrast between catholic theology and the thought of both Kant and Ritschl who, in their own ways, drew the circle around religious and moral experience. Underrate the religious importance of the "thing-element", and it is good-bye to a sacramental view of the world and to a coherent view of revelation.

It was in a sense the "thing-element" in the world which mattered greatly to Thornton in every part of his work. He dwelt upon the utter dependence of the created world upon the Creator, and upon the sacramental significance of that world. This was the theme, treated with a lucidity for which several generations of students must be grateful, of his essay in *Essays Catholic and Critical*. It was also the theme of the great work, *The Incarnate Lord*, where an organic view of the world was expounded with the Incarnation as the climax. *The Incarnate Lord* is typically liberal-catholic in the attempt to ally traditional dogma to a contemporary philosophy; but it towers above other works of the kind by the success with which it avoids assimilating the historical revelation to the demands of the philosophical system. The thesis was criticized as involving the abandonment of the organic principle at the crucial point of the Incarnation itself, and substituting the idea of a "divine intruder" so as to imply a virtually Apollinarian Christology. I would say rather that it was at this very point that Thornton showed his success in *not* subordinating the essence of New Testament teaching to the tidiness of the philosophical pattern.

Within *The Incarnate Lord* there is a chapter, necessary indeed for the theme of the book, but also standing apart as a self-contained essay; it is on "The Word and the Spirit". Here we see Thornton in the rôle he was later to follow more conspicuously— the Biblical exegete. It is a superb treatment of the distinction within the New Testament between the Risen Christ and the

---

[1] *Richard Hooker*, p. 87.

Holy Spirit in the work of grace in the Christian life. Had this chapter been published alone, it would stand as among Thornton's finest works.

In the later twenties and thirties Thornton gave much mental energy to his membership of the Commission on Doctrine in the Church of England, an activity in which he thrived greatly, for he was always a theological talker, receiving and giving enjoyment in the cut and thrust of discussion. I think he lost much when the work of the Commission ended, and he became intellectually rather solitary; though in later years the conferences of the Fellowship of St Alban and St Sergius drew him happily into action. But after the thirties liberal catholicism declined. The changes in the scope and character of Thornton's work were a symbol of what was happening.

In *The Incarnate Lord* an attempt was made to relate the revelation of God in Christ to current philosophy. But now another problem presented itself. "What if the Gospel becomes obscured by our presuppositions and preoccupations, so that we neither see the scope of its application nor suffer it to speak for itself?" So wrote Thornton in the preface to *The Common Life in the Body of Christ* (1942). Readers of his earlier works were startled. Here was something so very different; no interplay of Biblical and philosophical categories, no critical analysis of the phases of Biblical thought, but a massive illustration of the method of interpreting scripture by scripture. It was a feast of Biblical study, sending the reader to and fro between Synoptists, St Paul, St John, and the rest. It did not employ to any large extent the typological methods which were to become a disconcerting feature of Thornton's work. It did, however, illustrate what was to remain his conviction for the rest of his life: that the thought-forms of Biblical language, both Hebrew and Greek, are an integral part of divine revelation, and that we need to get inside these thought-forms in order to grasp a Biblical "wholeness" which otherwise we miss.

Now began the years (from the early forties) which Thornton gave to poring over the Bible, soaking himself in it, and seeing a thousand connections never seen before. He became deep in typology. He did not clarify the principles on which he used it; he simply used it, confidently and ubiquitously. I was one of those rarely convinced, ready to say that eccentricity had crept into the working of his mind, and suspecting that he was not always quite serious. Most startling was his habit of invoking typology in the discussion of some current ecclesiastical problem. Thus, when discussing the relation of Baptism to Confirmation with a synod of clergy, Thornton startled them by appealing to the description of the circumcision of the Israelites in Joshua 5, where the phrase in the LXX, "sharp petrine swords", prefigures the two stages of Christian initiation. In the *Catholicity* group, papers were invited from the members to open up the examination of the relation between catholic and protestant thought. Thornton's paper began with the words, "The Rabbis had a tradition that Adam was of gigantic stature".

It was easy to be exasperated by these vagaries; but, amidst them, Thornton was saying much else besides—about the "wholeness" of the Bible in its witness to Christ, to the unity of creation and redemption, of the essence of revelation and its forms. It was in this context that Thornton gave much thought to problems of Christian Reunion, convinced that the prevailing modes of approach to it burked questions about revelation and authority which lay beneath matters of ecclesiology.

In 1951 there came the great work of Thornton's later period, *Revelation and the Modern World*. It showed that his mind had been engaged with a great deal more than the detection of types. Revelation does not merely transcend, or merely use as a temporary tool, the cultural environment in which it is set. It masters and transforms that environment by a process of condescension in *The Form of the Servant* (the name given to the trilogy of which *Revelation and the Modern World* is the first volume). There is thus a constant correlation between the redemptive process and the various responses to the Creator within the created world, and a constant taking up of the phases of man's religious and cultural activity into the service of revelation. To Thornton, the supreme apostasy was to pick congenial parts of the Biblical revelation and unite them with congenial parts of contemporary thought; that was the bogus synthesis of liberalism. Rather does the Bible show us a wholeness of revelation using the wholeness of contemporary cultures, and prefiguring the process required to-day; not a synthesis of selected parts, but a fearless proclaiming of the whole Gospel, and as fearless a will to use and to learn from *all* contemporary sciences which, if true, are correlative to the revelation.

The second and third volumes of the trilogy expand the thesis in closer relation to the mission of the Church and to the unity of the Bible, with some dubious pieces of typological exegesis. But the heart of the thesis is in the first volume. It stands with *The Incarnate Lord* and *The Common Life in the Body of Christ* as one of Thornton's three great works. There is a unity between the three of them, and in the last there is in a sense a reaffirmation of the theme of the first. But, whereas *The Incarnate Lord* shows us how we may think of the unity of revelation and the world if we employ a particular philosophy, *Revelation and the Modern World* shows us how that unity is best grasped in uncompromising Biblical terms which yet enable us to sit at the feet of any genuine science.

It has fallen to few theologians to resemble Thornton in belonging to two very different epochs in theological history, and to render distinguished service to both. He was among the greatest of the liberal catholics, with a remarkable freedom from some of the acknowledged faults of that period. He became a supreme exponent of the Biblical theology in reaction from the liberal phase. If he showed some of the more tiresome and less convincing features of that reaction in his typological excursions, he had also a rare ability to recapture the mental interests of his earlier life and show, more comprehensively than in his earlier life, how Biblical faith and modern knowledge can go together.

It is impossible to separate Lionel Thornton the theologian from Lionel Thornton the man. His mind was complex, like a great machine in which many different things were going on all at once; and I believe that his attention to philosophical questions continued in the midst of his apparent absorption in "types". He was also extraordinarily simple, with a child's *naïveté*. As a preacher and a conductor of retreats—and I cannot doubt as a guide of souls—he had a simplicity and directness, always there in the heart of the man and in the heart of his theology. His devotion to the Community, which was to him home and family from the day of his profession, was an epitome of his devotion of heart and mind to the unity of God and man.

Herbert Kelly: Prophet

I knew Herbert Kelly only when he was a very old man and very deaf, though he had been deaf for a long time. I think that at first sight anyone would describe him as a funny old fellow, and in a sort of way he had for long years been a funny old fellow. My first encounter with him gave me an odd impression of a man full of ideas, some of them hard at first to grasp, and at the same time right down to earth. What he was doing, when I first met him, was chopping wood; and it was very clear that while his head was full of great ideas he was also giving himself with zest and enthusiasm to the chopping of the wood, as if chopping wood was the very thing that man was created to do. And of course it is exactly what man was created to do, along with some other things.

Now Herbert Kelly was a boy at Manchester Grammar School. Nothing odd in that! Then he went up to Oxford. Nothing odd in that! And then he was ordained and became a clergyman. Nothing odd in *that*! But it struck him at the time that it was a great pity that the clergy of the Church of England, as he came across them, seemed by and large to be comfortable, fairly well-to-do men, from the class of society that has got enough money to send itself up to one of the universities. It struck him as being a great pity that this was so, and his heart was full of the vision that the service of Christ in the ordained ministry *demanded* men of any and every part of the community, ready to strip themselves of property, strip themselves of comfort, and to go just anywhere in the service of Christ and of his Church, giving up their own wills in total allegiance and obedience.

This vision involved two things that went closely together. One was that more men be called to the priesthood from parts of the community from which priests seemed very seldom to come. The other was a certain *quality* of vocation that he longed to see in them, in himself, and in all who served the Church of God. And this quality of vocation demanded for some (I am quoting almost his own words) to work without pay, to remain unmarried, and to be obedient. And by being obedient he meant a kind of life in which not only the big critical choices, but the daily deciding what you do and how you spend your time is based not on what "I like and feel inclined" but upon obedience to a will which somehow represents for you the will of Christ himself. This spirit of obedience meant in his belief a real death to self. Fr Kelly used to say that in the martyrs of the early Church the thing that counted was not the impression they made on the world by their martyrdom, not the things that they themselves said about it, but just the act of obedience, the self given completely to the will of God.

From Fr Kelly's vision there came about a brotherhood. The original purpose of the brotherhood was to go and work in Korea. In fact they did not go and work in Korea, though some of them went and worked in Central Africa. And that uncertainty as to what exactly they were going to do, and the fact that the first project (so to speak) misfired, is rather characteristic of the man and the thing. Not laying down for themselves exactly what the project was to be, but rather forming an idea and an ideal and waiting upon God to discover the form which ultimately it would take. And ultimately it took the form of the Society of the Sacred Mission which was, from the first, both a society and a college; a society of men pledged by vows to the service of Christ in poverty, celibacy, and obedience, and a college of men being trained for the priesthood in the atmosphere of those ideals which the society of monks was making its own.

In 1903 there took place the move from Mildenhall in Suffolk to Kelham near Newark on Trent, which has been the home of the Society ever since. And if you travel north to south on the Great North Road, or if you go by train from London to York, just outside Newark you look across the fields for a mile or two and you see a great big country house of rather odd neo-gothic architecture, for all the world extraordinarily like St Pancras Station. But it is not all that kind of architecture, which the friends of

Kelham both laugh at and love so dearly, because besides the older building there is the very beautiful chapel built in 1928. The chapel seems wonderfully to escape the different conventionalisms in which church architecture gets itself involved through the centuries, and while touching the modern age seems to be timeless in its representation of the austerity and at the same time the tenderness of our Christian faith. And that is Kelham. There, at that place, the Society has gone on living and praying; and the college has gone on, and from it I don't know how many young men have been sent out into the ranks of the priesthood imbued with its ideals. And time would fail me to tell of the other work of the community in parishes in England, in Africa, and in Australia.

Herbert Kelly served the Church and the world by what he taught. And what he taught was theology. When he said theology he meant something very distinctive and not quite the same as what a lot of other people have meant when they use the word. The order of the day used to be that the mentally adequate man who was a candidate for holy orders first went and took a degree at a university and then added to that a theological college course. To that system the Church of England and the bishops of the day were very wedded. Fr Kelly criticized that and provided his alternative, not as a sort of poor relation to the established system, but because he believed that the established system called for radical criticism. And this is the criticism he made of it again and again. He used to say,

> You send these bright young men to the universities, where they get a secular education and learn about the secular world in a secular way; and when they have done that you give them some theology as a kind of top-dressing. As a result they have not really made sense of the secular world and secular studies, because they have not had theology as a standard by which to judge it. And equally when they do their theology they find it in a sort of vacuum unrelated to the previous secular studies.

It was a very shrewd criticism.

Fr Kelly's own plan was the long Kelham course which he

founded and developed, in which you study (if you have the good fortune to be there) theology and a lot of secular subjects so inter-related that you are able to see how the very course of the world has itself got theological roots, how theology makes sense when it is brought to bear on the secular world and its studies, the whole forming some kind of unity. The criticism was, "Yet get these men all in a kind of monastery, bottled up; is it not very narrow for them?" And Fr Kelly had his answer to that criticism in a single sentence, "We teach them to think". And I believe he did teach them to think, and I believe that Kelham still does teach them to think. For all those reasons I believe that, both in his critique of the educational assumptions of the time and in his working out an educational programme both cultural and theo-logical, Fr Kelly was one of the great educationalists of the time.

But we still have not said what he meant when he used the word theology. Kelly was a disciple of a great teacher of the last century, F. D. Maurice, and if I give you one sentence from F. D. Maurice the point will come clear at once. Maurice said this: "We have been dosing the people with religion when what they need is not religion but the living God." Not our thoughts about religion, our attitude to God, what we make of God, what we feel about God, what we formulate intellectually about God; all those things, though so necessary, are inadequate. It is not this that we must try to convey to the people of the country. No, it is the living God himself, to which all these things are pointers and witnesses but always inadequate pointers and witnesses.

Now that in essence is what Fr Kelly went on saying again and again. Let me quote to you remarks he made from time to time, at the S.C.M. conferences at Swanwick. "What does God *do*? Does God do anything, or is God only a name for our ideals?" "There used to be a thing called theology, it was about God. Now we have a thing called psychology of religion, and it's all about your own nice feelings." That is Kelly in a nutshell. Of course it raises questions as well as answering them, but no harm in that! The weight of his influence was upon the distinction between the living God and man's thoughts and feelings about him. Thus to Fr

Kelly dogma mattered enormously, but not as something to be idolized as a rigid system, but because dogma is merely a necessary but inadequate witness to the living God. The Bible matters supremely, but not something itself to be worshipped as a kind of self-contained article, because it is the witness to the Word who is God himself, the living and the true. The Sacraments matter supremely, but not something to be propagandized about as things in themselves, because they are really (I think he would dare to say) nothing of themselves, witnessing to and finding their fullness only in the living God.

As a result of this tremendous emphasis upon the living God, two practical things followed in Fr Kelly's teaching and influence. First, he was able to cut through the kind of idea that God is interested only in religion and that the only way of getting near to God is by being "pious" in the conventional sense. Very characteristically, a book of reminiscences of Fr Kelly just published has the title *No Pious Person*. "God is as interested in the pigs that you are feeding or the bus that you are driving as he is in you when you fold your hands and say prayers to him." The depth of the conviction of the living God cuts through to the grasp that everything secular is near to God just because he is so living.

The second consequence was Fr Kelly's approach to unity. When once the conviction of the living God is on top and felt to be far greater than theological systems about him, then it is possible, without necessarily in the least wanting to disparage or disavow your own theological system, to find yourself in living contact with Christians of any and every kind. And I think it was thus that Fr Kelly found himself thrown into that ecumenical and interdenominational contact of minds and spirits which in the earlier years of this century operated so largely within the Student Christian Movement. In fact, an immense exchange of minds and ideas happened and was liberated, because Fr Kelly was getting all the time to something deeper and greater than our ideas about God. So it was that he came to be described as a man who wonderfully combined the virtues of the Catholic and the Protestant.

One more thing. Because of his conviction about the living God, Kelly always used to say that great people and wonderful people and saintly people did not matter as much, and anyhow did not interest him as much, as just ordinary people, just anybody. To illustrate that, and to illustrate Fr Kelly's wonderful way of expounding the Bible, I want to give you a quotation. At the time there was a lot of talk about different parts of the Bible being very inspired and other parts were rather disparaged as of a lower level of inspiration. So Fr Kelly for this exposition seized on about one of the most unpromising-looking passages he could find, a genealogy in the book of Chronicles. He said,

"And Azariah begat Helas and Helas begat Eleazar . . ." and so on we go to Shermat and Shallum in about fifty columns: what you boys call a low degree of inspiration. Who are these people and what are they doing in the Bible? Well, they are like another passage, "Eliud begat another Eleazar, and Eleazar begat Matthan, and Matthan begat Jacob . . ."; and there was a Welsh quarryman who prayed, "Lord, thou knowest I cannot pronounce these names, so I will call them Williams and Jones and Roberts". Yes, ordinary, unseen people like you and me, and very probably they also had a low degree of inspiration, carrying on just as they could while God was preparing in his own good time, "Jacob begat Joseph, the husband of Mary, of whom was born Jesus who is called the Christ". Immanuel. God-with-us.

That was how Kelly thought about human life, that was how he expounded the Bible, and that was what he meant by theology. "Little men, little men, little men, all going through the ages in a procession, but alongside them all the greatness of God." Not our thoughts about him, however bright; not our dogmas about him, however correct; not our prayers to him, however pious; but God, God the living and the true.

Well, Fr Kelly, knowing that men were little and that God was great, gave up the directorship of Kelham, feeling that it was his calling to ask questions and to probe and to set people thinking, and the calling of other people to do the ruling and the directing. So he became the Old Man, and in due time he died. He died on the eve of All Saints Day 1950, and he went to his account like Eliud and Eleazar and Matthan and Williams and Jones and Roberts, and all the rest of them. "What is man that thou art mindful of him?" But this man, a man astonished out of his wits and shaking with laughter at the thought that we were commemorating him in a great hall in his birthplace, this little man bore witness to the truth of the living God, and so was able to teach his contemporaries and go on perhaps teaching all of us this: that the living God is near to every single thing that is happening in our world, and also that the service of the living God, whatever outward form it takes, calls for the total surrender of the will, a real dying to self, that Christ may reign in us. And, being dead, Herbert Kelly yet speaketh; and does not our Church need to get back to what he teaches us—the reality of the living God, so that there is an unlimited catholicity in the Church's will to relate everything to God? But of that catholicity there is always a price, and the price is that in the heart of the Church's life there shall be the renunciation of the world and the self for God's own sake and glory. "Lord, grant what thou commandest, and command what thou wilt."

George Bell

Thine eyes shall see the king in his beauty:
they shall behold a far stretching land.
                                        Isa. 33.17

To-day a great gathering of Christian people from Chichester,
from Sussex, and from far beyond commemorates with gratitude a much-loved man, Christian and bishop. Of George Bell's
many gifts it may fairly be said that in his public life the most
conspicuous gift was *courage*, in his personal character the most
striking was *humility*, and in his mental equipment the most
creative was *imagination*. Imagination perceives beauty and
interprets it, imagination distinguishes great things from small,
and imagination ranges wide in sympathy and understanding. It
has the eye which, in the prophetic words of my text, sees the
king in his beauty and roves over far stretching lands.

Here in the Cathedral we remember George Bell's love for
beauty. He had in his years as Dean of Canterbury used wonderfully his care for a beautiful house of God, with its liturgy, its
worship, its welcome. He had shown his concern that drama
should recover its right place in the service of the Christian message. These gifts he brought to Chichester, and who did more
than he to foster throughout our Church the conserving and creating of things beautiful? To-day's restoration of the Arundel
Screen in the Cathedral is an act which both restores beauty and
creates it, and can we doubt that this is near to his heart?

It was with a like imagination that George Bell distinguished
things great and things small. A very capable administrator he did
not allow his mind to be absorbed by such matters. He saw issues
in big ways: the unity of the Church, the liberty of the Church
of England to control its own life and reform its own worship,

the presentation of the Gospel in the face of the mental problems of an age of science, the peril to the world of the new destructive weapons, the duty of the prosperous nations towards those which are poor and hungry, and all the while the primacy of the worship of God for his own glory's sake. To George Bell's imagination the great things of faith and duty stood out plain to see, like mighty mountain peaks in a land of far distances.

Imagination is, however, not of the mind alone; it includes the understanding heart. Such was George Bell's feeling, caring, sharing over the far distances of human need. Quickly he felt for the persecuted Christians of Europe, and became their friend for ever. In his quest of unity he understood different Christian traditions, Protestant, Orthodox, Roman, in their piety, their feelings, their prejudices, their history. And in those legions of human relationships which fill any man's life, and not least the life of a pastor, he entered into *your* feelings, he saw what the matter in hand meant to *you*.

So, to the service of God and man George Bell brought a rare natural gift of imagination; and in God's service how wonderfully was it enriched—in the vision of beauty, in the perception of great issues, and in far-stretching sympathy! There have been great men whose love of beauty has been isolated from a concern for humanity in its rough and ugly distress. There have been great men too whose concern for humanity has missed the vision of heavenly things beyond. Here in Chichester was a man for whom that cleavage was impossible. To him the vision of the king in his beauty, and the vision of a far-stretching land of human trial and sorrow went always together. To-day we thank God for him, whose loss to us is no less grievous as time passes and whose message to us is no less urgent; and we pray that God of his goodness will give to us a portion of his spirit. St Thomas à Kempis said: "The sons of God standing upon the things that are present do contemplate those things which are eternal. They look on transitory things with the left eye, and with the right they see the things of heaven." Thanking God for one who had both eyes open and alert we pray that ours may not be closed.

PASTORALIA

Retreats:
Their Aim and Conduct

THE MEANING OF RETREAT

I am to speak to you about the meaning of Retreat, for the world, for the Christian, and for the Church.

When pleas are made about the desirability of Retreat, many characteristics of our contemporary age are alluded to, as, for instance, that it is noisy and bustling and tiring. My diagnosis would be to use the word "overcrowded"—our age is overcrowded, and in particular the mind and heart of man are overcrowded. Each day a man or a woman does so many things, sees so many things, hears so many things, says so many things, and the mind has crowded into it a multitude of impressions, flitting in and out. Some are important, others are unimportant. Some are good, some are bad. Some are worth preserving, some are merely of the moment. Some are worth pausing to consider, others are worth no consideration at all. Yet the mind and the heart are so overcrowded by this rapidity of sensations that for millions of people the power is lost to distinguish, to reflect, to reject, or to approve thoughtfully, rationally, conscientiously. The power is lost to do what St Paul calls, "to approve the things that are excellent".

It follows that purely from a humanist point of view, because man is so overcrowded in heart and mind, he is frustrated from being his own best self through a constant servitude to the haphazard. It is the reign of the haphazard that is so diabolical. From a theological point of view we can put the diagnosis a bit differently and say this: that man is the slave of the temporal flux of events, sensations, experiences, and therefore he misses the realization of himself as a child of eternity. "There was silence in heaven." "Be still, and know that I am God." But man being enslaved to the temporal flux, fails to be able to "consider", in the Biblical meaning of that word. Remember the very significant and telling way in which the word "consider" is used in the Bible. "Consider the lilies, how they grow." And they grow in a very leisurely way and if you are to consider how they grow you must have some affinity to their leisureliness. "When I consider the heavens, even the works of thy hands, what is man that thou art mindful of him?" "O, consider this, ye that forget God." The power to "consider" is undermined.

When therefore we talk about Retreat we are saying something that touches the plight of the world in which we are living. It is not only that the heart and mind of man is so liable to be overcrowded by much that is bad, but that when good things are present in the mind man lacks the power to realize them to himself, to enjoy them, consider them, and treasure them.

What then is the rôle of the Church? The Church is commissioned by her Lord to be living in the midst of the world a life Godward in worship and adoration, a life manward in the service of humanity and in the carrying of the Gospel of God to it. And thus the Church's life, Godward and manward, is a constant rhythm of coming and going, detachment and involvement.

When the Church fails it is because the spirit of the world in one way or another invades it, and indeed every member of the Church has his double existence of flesh and spirit. He is still a member of the created world where sin is rampant, while being also a member of the divine order of the resurrection. And historians of the Church are never slow to point out how in particular ages of the Church the spirit of the world has invaded it in this or that evil way. To-day, it seems to me that the spirit of the world has invaded the Church in a very distressing way by the disease of this mental and spiritual overcrowding of which I was speaking. There are so many things that the Church must do. Every priest is doing things day by day and week by week, and then he discovers that if he were a better priest there would be still more things for

146

him to be doing. Every faithful layman is doing innumerable things in the service of God, day by day and week by week, and from time to time his conscience is stirred to see that there are more things that urgently need to be done, and to set himself to them. And thus the Church, engaging with a world which is more and more complex, finds itself involved on every front and constantly discovering and opening up more and more new fronts on which to fight. What follows? One result is that amidst this faithful doing by the Church of the Church's hard work there is the overcrowding of the Church's mind and soul. So it is that we who belong to the Church succumb to the world's characteristic disease of being dominated by the flux of time and of losing the power to "consider".

THE CONDUCT OF A RETREAT

I speak now about the Retreat and its conductor. I believe that there is a true simplicity in his task. A priest may shrink from conducting Retreats through a feeling that it means leading people in some specialized, higher flights of spirituality, and therefore the quest is not for him. But what is it that in fact is asked of him?

1. He must be ready to speak quite simply about the great verities of the Christian faith so that the retreatants can absorb what he says.

2. He must have pastoral sympathy, such as he needs in any part of his office and ministry.

3. He must himself be a man of Retreat, who loves to see other Christian folk finding something which he himself has found by going to Retreat—some words of St Dominic put this: "contemplata aliis tradere".

It is important that far more priests should feel that conducting a Retreat is a natural thing for them to do, and the competence is really not beyond their reach. There is no special sort of spiritual "diploma" between them and this particular work.

The aim of a Retreat is the realization of God by a Christian soul. This can happen in as many ways as there are Christian souls. It means the realization of *God in himself*—his majesty, eternity, love, nearness, tenderness, bounty, righteousness. It means also, for each retreatant, the realization of something of *God's will for me*. The realization can take a number of forms. It may sometimes be the realization of his will that I should love him more, remember him more, and pray better. It may sometimes be a specific resolution that I shall do this or that, or be in this or that respect a better man. The emphasis upon God's *will* must always issue from a Retreat, just because God is righteous. But this emphasis upon God's will comes in the context of realizing God himself, his being, his presence. It is this which makes the difference between a Retreat and a moral leadership course.

This aim, the realization of God, now subdivides into two aspects which are often contrasted. Books about Retreat, and the approach of different conductors, are apt to dwell upon one or other of these aspects:

1. There is the passive aspect of a Retreat. We are familiar with this in the prayers of R. M. Benson, often used at the opening of a Retreat, when we pray that we may "rest awhile at this present time with thee", or in the Compline prayer that we may "rest upon thine eternal changelessness". In this way it is possible to present a Retreat in terms of having a rest, enjoying a cessation of all the normal busyness of life, and getting away from the flux of coming and going, of talking and doing, and amidst the silence resting upon the "strength and stay upholding all creation who ever dost thyself unmoved abide".

2. On the other hand, a Retreat can be presented as a time of strenuous activity. The phrase used is "to *make* a retreat". Those who share in it are called "exercitants". They are told that they have not come to sit and do nothing. They are to use their wills in mental exercise, in decision, in self-offering. They have come to do some hard work by God's grace.

This contrast, which I have deliberately put in sharp terms, is likely to appear in our discussions here. It corresponds partly, but only partly, with the contrast between the Ignatian and the Benedictine approaches; the one leads the soul through a path of exercises, the other brings the soul near to God trusting that he will do with it what he wills. I do not believe that the two ways of looking at it are mutually exclusive. Let me describe the way in which I incline to think of a Retreat as a result of my own experience.

I think of it in the first place as "having a good rest". I tell the retreatants that they are here to *enjoy* a rest, to be without all the things which normally preoccupy and tire and worry. Have a rest. Go deep into the relaxation and peace of silence. But there is no such thing as emptiness. God is here. More and more in the silence you will realize, God is here. It will be a rest *towards God*. *Vacate Deo.* He will be drawing you towards himself; let the imagination, the desire, respond towards him. Then there will come the activities of love, of imagination, of prayer. But it will still be rest; for God is perfect rest. Amid the energies of his righteous will, overflowing in his gifts and tremendous in his demands, there is a divine peace and rest all around us.

How then will the conductor serve this aim which we have been describing?

1. He will give addresses. These must be short. They must also be about the great Christian verities. Whatever plan is followed, or titles are given, the addresses must be about that. God, majestic, the Creator, loving: Our Lord, incarnate, risen, crucified, the Holy Spirit: my creation, my vocation, my sins, my Saviour, my God. Such must, in one way or another, be the themes, because the aim is the realization of God. The addresses must also be sympathetic, with the note of "what these things mean to you". Let is also be remembered that whereas in parochial preaching you often have to drive the theme home, in Retreat you can more easily let it quietly find its own way home. The quietness, the atmosphere of the Retreat, helps what is spoken gently to come home to the imagination and the conscience. Amongst the themes, that of "God my Creator" inevitably comes to be prominent in Retreat, because there is the greatest possibility in quietness of realizing the fundamental truth about ourselves. "Thy hands have made me and fashioned me."

2. The conductor will help the retreatants to meditate and to pray in response to the great verities of which he speaks in the addresses. Here, his aim will be to evoke, to suggest, to set the retreatants the way of praying, which they will do each in his own way. I believe that it is very valuable for the conductor to lead the retreatants in *acts* of faith, hope, love, penitence, thanksgiving— such acts as "O my God I love thee: help me to love thee more". Such acts give scope for the "affective" element in prayer which has too little scope in the ordinary round of Church worship. I distrust "conducted meditations"; they are sometimes first cousins to the "long prayer" of the Presbyterian kirk.

3. The conductor will remember that Retreat concerns the individual soul being alone with God, and he will avoid attempts at "corporateness" of an inappropriate kind. At the present time the note of "corporateness" is very prominent in parochial life, and rightly so. But it is a big mistake (occasionally made) to try and transport into a parochial retreat the "all-togetherness" of normal parochial life. The aim of the Retreat is to enable the individual soul to find itself alone with God and to listen to what he may say concerning *me*. How rare are the opportunities for this. So do not fill the Retreat with corporate language and say "we" this and "we" that; do not clutter up the Retreat with intercessions. Yet there is, all the time, the strength which is brought to the Retreat through the fact that it is within the Church's common life. The Eucharist, the offices, enable the realization of this—the liturgical background of the Church's prayer, sustaining, refreshing, liberating. That is where the corporateness comes in. It enables the self-realization of the soul with God which is the goal of the Retreat: "Thy hands have made *me* and fashioned *me*." "He loved *me* and gave himself for *me*." "My son, give me *thine* heart."

4. Though the goal is different with every retreatant, there is a common aim which the conductor has before him, that all may find the presence of God and be led through the stages of adoration, penitence, peace of soul, the will to serve God better. The conductor will be in general conscious of "how the retreat is

going"; there is a spiritual rhythm, an atmosphere which is often vividly sensed. The conductor will be aware, broadly, of what is happening both from this sense of "rhythm" and from the talks which some of the retreatants may have with him about themselves. But it is not for him to know, or to worry, about what is happening in the soul of each and every retreatant, still less to think that he is there, so to speak, to "put them through it". He is there as *servus servorum Dei*.

I give you these suggestions about the aim of a Retreat, and about the rôle of the conductor. A word, finally, of how people will be led to go into Retreat. Only the leisured can go for three or four days in the middle of a week, or those who spare some days from a holiday. Increasingly it is the parochial week-end Retreats which are in our minds. It may be best on the first occasion of a parochial week-end to have not a Retreat, but a time for instruction, devotion, and recreation. But when the definite step of a first Retreat is arranged *let the silence be complete throughout*. It is no help or kindness to provide interludes for talking in the hope of relieving the strain of silence for beginners; rather do such interludes make the strain more difficult. The only initiation into silence is silence; and it is when silence is unbroken by conversation that the strain can yield to unselfconscious enjoyment of silence in depth.

THE OUTCOME OF RETREAT

Who can tell what the outcome may be for each retreatant? There may be many kinds of realizations and resolutions. But I believe we may always hope that the one outcome will be a greater possession of the spirit of Retreat in daily life—the spirit of "be still, and know that I am God".

So what may the greater practice of Retreat do for the Church? It can bring into the midst of the Church's ceaseless activity something of that passivity which belongs to the realization of the presence of God among us. Fénelon in a letter to a French duke of his time, wrote this: "I want to help you to find how to lead *a very full and yet a leisurely life.*" Our Church has a very full life, a life overcrowded with its own multiple activities. Retreat can give to our Church, involved as it is in the temporal order in a very full life, also a truly leisurely life—a life nearer to the true norm of "contemplare et contemplata aliis tradere". The members of the Church will know that it is of the essence of their calling "vacare Deo", "vacare considerationi".

Let me end by reading a letter of Baron von Hügel, which sums up all, sums up not only the spirit in which a Retreat may be approached but also the meaning of it for the whole life of the Church.

26 October 1920. No doubt a Retreat depends somewhat on the giver of it; yet it really depends far more upon the simplicity and generosity of the soul that makes the Retreat. I am sure you already know well that you must evade all straining, all vehemence, all as it were putting your nerves into it. On the contrary the attention wanted is leisurely expansion, a gentle dropping of distractions, of obsessions. That is the instrument of progress, the recipient of graces. This old scribbler, how much of that dropping, evading, gently waiting, (as against his interior vehemences and uproar, a sterile and sterilizing restlessness) he has to practice. Yet the practice shows him plainly that *that* is what good sense and God want of him. Peace and power come that way and only that way. I know too that you should never strain, never directly strive to like people, just merely drop or ignore your antipathies . . . Meanwhile they keep us humble and watchful and close to God. I am so glad you begin your Retreat on All Saints, my favourite feast—the feast not only of all the heroic lovers of God that have ever lived, but the feast of single heroic supernatural acts, even if and where they remain single.[1]

[1] *Selected Letters 1896–1924*, p. 314.

The Monastic Life

Show thy servants thy work: and their children their glory.
Ps. 90.16

It is a happy thing that to-day's ceremony here takes place at a time when the hearts of Christian people with a sense of history are moved by the commemoration of St Hilda and her foundation of the Abbey at Whitby thirteen hundred years ago. In his fascinating book, *Leaders in the Northern Church*, Bishop Lightfoot drew a parallel between Hilda in seventh-century England and Deborah in the age of the Judges in Canaan. Both women "arose a mother in Israel" to bring unity to the people and to do battle in the name of God. Both were women of fiery energy and royal spirit. But their weapons were very different. Hilda, though she was the child of a race of warriors and bore the name of a Saxon war-goddess, had love as her weapon and peacefulness as her warfare. She conquered, spreading the peace of Christ in a time of cruelty and division.

To-day, therefore, we pause to give thanks to God for his servant Hilda. The niece of King Edwin, she received the faith and the sacraments from St Paulinus; she never wavered in her faith despite the pagan reaction and the withdrawal of the Kentish mission, she embraced the monastic life under St Aidan's direction, she ruled in turn the monasteries at Hartlepool and Whitby; women and men were both under her rule, five bishops were among the men whom she trained. "She brought about", says Bede, "the amendment and salvation of many living far distant, who heard the inspiring story of her industry and goodness." "To her", says Bede again, "kings and princes came to ask her counsel in their troubles." The last seven years of her life were stricken with illness and pain, and through them her ministry of private counsel and public teaching continued—until the day when "she summoned all the servants of Christ in the monastery, and urged them to maintain the gospel peace among themselves and with others", and "while she was still speaking she joyfully welcomed death, and in the words of our Lord passed from death to life".

We thank God for Hilda to-day. We thank God for her catholicity—no faction could claim her: her service was to God and his whole Church in the land. We thank God for her service to culture; for her faith bore fruit in a love for art and letters as gifts of the good Creator, and a touching symbol of this is the story of the coming of the poet Caedmon to Whitby to learn from Hilda to sing in epic verse the mighty deeds of God in the Bible. But a claim to our thanksgiving still more explicit, still more distinctive, remains. To Hilda belonged that threefold vocation to poverty, chastity, and obedience under the threefold vow which makes the monastic life. That God has called men and women to serve him in this particular calling, for his glory, for the good of his Church, and for the fulfilment of Christian precepts—for this we give grateful thanks and praise. In the lives of many who have followed this vocation, God has shown his servants his work and their children his glory.

Centuries pass. The shape of civilizations changes and changes again. Still, the Church of England continues, the Catholic and Apostolic Church in this land. Many are the marks of her continuity; and among these not the least is the revival of the vocation to the service of God in communities under the threefold vow. We thank God for this revival; and herein especially we thank God for the Order of the Holy Paraclete. In the forty years of its existence it has been used of God in many good works; in the teaching of the Christian faith in northern England, and in Africa too—where the sisters now at work have to-day our very special remembrance, for the days are evil and it is not easy to redeem the time. But, beneath all that the Community does in teaching and in the fostering of Christian culture, there is the secret of the monastic life, the adoration of God in worship and prayer for God's own sake and glory. "Seven times a day do I praise thee,

O Lord." "I will magnify thee, O God my King, and I will praise thy name for ever and ever. Every day will I give thanks unto thee, and praise thy name for ever and ever." Herein God shows his work to his servants.

To-day every friend of the Community—and we are many—rejoices at the completion and consecration of this very beautiful Chapel. The old Chapel had indeed its hold upon our hearts, and within it God showed his work to his servants, and his glory to many children. But here the Community now worships with greater space and greater light, and his glorious majesty will rest upon them. He has been very good to us, and we thank him with our hearts. But as we thank him we find his voice speaking to our consciences. What does it to-day say to us? Perhaps it reminds us that the particular vocation of monk or nun to poverty, chastity, and obedience is but one form of the vocation every single Christian has at his baptism: to be poor in spirit, to be pure in heart, to be obedient to the Lord Jesus. This vocation belongs to each one of us, and it bids each one of us search his heart before Our Lord "who loved me and gave himself for me". Thanking and praising God for his mighty deeds in the conversion of our land of old, for his goodness and bounty to our greatly loved Order of the Holy Paraclete, for this house now built for his worship, we pray that he will raise up his power and come among us for our sanctification and for the winning of souls.

The Priest

He leadeth them up into a high mountain apart by
themselves, and he was transfigured before them.

Mark 9.2

Our festival to-day sends each one of us back to the days we first
spent here at Cuddesdon, and evokes from each of us a gratitude
searching and specific. How do we describe what Cuddesdon
meant to us? It was here that we came to know and to love, each
in his own time, those who taught and guided and inspired us. It
was here that the ideal of what it means to be a priest came vividly
home to us. It was here that we faced the truth about ourselves
before the Cross of Christ, and with the painful shattering of our
pride discovered that we have no sufficiency of ourselves to think
anything of ourselves. And, with memories solemn and searching,
there mingle memories light and ludicrous, since, for all the
seriousness of the purpose which brought us here, we were here
as human beings with our absurdities and our sense of the absurd.
Learning to laugh at ourselves, we did not lack other things to
laugh about. How should we, if the Christian life is indeed the
knowledge of him who is the author of laughter as well as tears?

Is it fanciful to see in what Cuddesdon meant to us a little
re-enactment of the story of the Transfiguration? We were, in a
way that was novel and alarming, "apart by ourselves". We were
withdrawn. We were faced with what Newman calls the "two
luminously clear realities: the soul and its creator". We were
apart, too, as men climbing a mountain. The discipline was not
easy for all of us. Learning to pray is difficult. Learning theology
is difficult. But we were apart, and climbing, because we believed
that our Lord was so leading us. And he was leading us in order
that he might give us, here on the sacred hill, a glimpse of his

glory. Moses and Elijah—our study of the Scriptures—helped us by their own witness; but our study of the Scriptures was done to the end that our Lord might show himself to us—Jesus glorious before his Passion. In contrition, in love, in gratitude we were glad that we had come, we were glad to be where we were, and we often said so: "It is good for us to be here." And then the cloud—the conviction of the presence of God, the cloud that enveloped all, became very real to us: "Deus fascinans, Deus tremendus." Then from the cloud there comes the voice, "Hear ye him". It was brought home to us that our God is not only to be adored; he is the righteous God, to be heard and obeyed, for never in the Christian dispensation is there the authentic cloud of the divine presence without the voice of the divine command: "Hear ye him." "Hear and obey." "Whatsoever he saith unto you, do it." We heard that voice. And we came down from the mountain.

In the years that have passed since we were here, the weirdest changes have been happening in the conditions under which our ministry is discharged—and this is true whatever our date may be, whether it was forty years ago, or thirty, or twenty or even ten years, or five. In my day—a generation now just a little elderly, though not yet senile—I doubt if any of us would have guessed that there would be a second world war within just over a decade, or that Communist Russia was destined to become so dark a menace to the world, or that vast movements of population in this country were going to alter the shape of our pastoral work. Nor could we have guessed the extent to which industrial development was going to bring about the technological kind of outlook as the mental ethos of so many of the people, nor that the Welfare State would really come to be, and when it came, would produce the mentality of comfort in the way it has. And who would have guessed that the epoch of social security within the State would also be the epoch of "near-catastrophe" in the world as a whole through the creation of weapons able to annihilate the world itself? The saying of Charles Gore, "There ain't no new thought: there ain't nothing new", seems now less obviously convincing than it did when first we heard him say it.

Faced by these vast changes, we find that the pattern of our ministry has had in many ways to change. In some of those changes, in spite of all that has distressed us, God has been wonderfully with us. Our congregations, never large in relation to the total population around us, are often more convinced in their allegiance, more instructed, more responsible, and above all more like the *ecclesia of God* realizing itself week by week as one bread, one body, in the eucharistic offering. Our laity are discovering that they must be the evangelists, penetrating the community of their neighbours with their own conviction of the Christian faith. But all the while, over against us, a mental outlook is created in the people of the country by TV, radio, newspapers, novels, and the rest—a mental background in which life and death, birth and marriage, home and work are discussed and argued about with the assumption that God and religion have no place whatever on the map. It is to penetrate this world of assumptions so far removed from the Christian faith that is our baffling task. Coming down from the mountain, we face indeed a faithless generation, with its dumb spirits, dashing it down so that it foameth and grindeth its teeth.

So new and strange are the times, that within the Church of God there is the recognition of the need for "something new". "Something new." New pastoral techniques, new modes of evangel, new ways of training our priests; and this last plea has been put in very picturesque language, that we must not try to fight a modern war with horse transport and with bows and arrows. What do we say to this plea?

"Something new" indeed there must be. I mention some needs which seem to me to be very urgent.

1. Within both the parishes and the industries of the land we need groups of laity trained as "cells" of the ecclesia, such as yet embody the ecclesia in themselves, meeting, studying, praying, looking for the will of God for themselves in the setting of their daily occupations, and drawing their neighbours into their fellowship. This is happening. It needs to happen more, not just as a

sort of "supernumerary extra", but as part of the normal ecclesiology of our time.

2. Again we need far more grappling with the influence of
radio and television in moulding the mental outlook of the people.
The Church as a whole must learn far more of the use of these
techniques, and in the parishes the priest and congregation must
know more of what their neighbours are watching and discussing,
and must be prepared to meet it and expose it.

3. Again, in the realm of theology, we need to break away
from the notion, which still clings, that theology and the humani-
ties are together the one mental discipline for a Christian, and
that science is necessarily another world. We need theologians, if
God will give them to us, who will think and write of God and
man from the midst of those very mental disciplines which a
scientific age is creating. "Something new." Yes, these are in-
stances of "something new"; and badly we need it.

Yet when the apostles were grappling with the worst manifestation of evil they had yet confronted, the dumb spirits dashing
the poor boy to the ground, foaming and grinding his teeth—and
they longed no doubt for new techniques, since the techniques
whereby devils had once been subject to them now seemed of no
avail, "Why could not we cast him out?", our Lord, coming down
from the mountain, said only, "Bring him to me", and the only
technique he mentions in rebuking the apostles is the "science of
the saints": "This kind goeth not out save by prayer and fasting."
Amid methods old and methods new, alike amid bows and arrows
and the weapons of modern war, the art and science of Christ and
the apostles remains to learn and to practise, never to be taken as
granted, always to be painfully learnt—"Bring him to me", "This
kind goeth not out save by prayer".

It means *withdrawal*. And whatever new things we learn and do
—and I do not doubt they are many and urgent—let none of them
blind us to the recurring need of withdrawal to the Mount. That
withdrawal must have its place in the training of our priests.
"Jesus chose twelve, that they might be with him." "Come ye
apart into a desert place and rest awhile: have leisure awhile."

"He brought them to a high mountain apart by themselves." I do not see this withdrawal exaggerated in the life of our Church, or in the counsels of our Church in its search for divine wisdom under the guidance of the Spirit. Rather does it seem all too widely forgotten and imperilled. To-day, for our own many failures in this, for our own forgetfulness of what Cuddesdon taught us, we ask forgiveness, and we ask for our renewal in the climbing of the holy mount.

"He brought them up to a high mountain, apart by themselves, and he was transfigured before them." It did not mean that he had left behind him the conflicts of the Galilean ministry which had gone before, or the conflicts of the Via Crucis which were to follow. That perhaps was St Peter's error, longing to linger in the glory of the mountain scene and to leave all that was irksome down below. Rather was it that, when our Lord went up to be transfigured, he carried with him every conflict, every burden, both of the days behind or the days ahead, to be transfigured with him. And when *we* go apart to be with Jesus in his glory, it is so that our frustrations, our pains, and our cares may be carried into that supernatural context which makes all the difference to them. These frustrations are not forgotten; they are not abolished; they can still be painful. But they become transfigured in the presence of Jesus, our crucified and glorious Lord. And when we have carried our frustrations up to our Lord in his glory, we find in the days which follow that he so generously brings his glory right down into the midst of our frustrations. "My peace I give unto you." "These things have I said unto you that my joy may be in you, and that your joy may be full." "Be of good cheer, I have overcome the world."

"It is good for us to be here." With grateful hearts we shall be taking leave of the place which means more to us than words can tell. But wherever we may be, we are still allowed to go apart by ourselves and to "climb" where we may see the glory of Jesus. And if we are really trying to do this, he is at hand to change us by his Spirit into the same image from glory to glory.

The Bishop

His servants shall serve him, and they shall see his face.

Rev. 22.3–4

To-day's act of installation of a bishop is set within the commemoration throughout all Christendom of the saints of God.
Our thoughts turn first towards them. While all Christians are
called to be saints, and are saints indeed through the presence of
the Holy Spirit within them, Christendom holds in honour those
men and women in whom saintliness has been supremely seen.
And wherein does saintliness really lie? What is it? The saint is
not just the virtuous person or the person who does good in the
world, though both these things may be true of him. Rather is the
saint one who is so genuinely near to God that a rare humility
marks him and enables him to convey to others the sense of God's
nearness. His virtues do not make him proud, for he is always
longing for the divine perfection far beyond them; and his sins
and failings—which may be many and bitter—humble him again
so that God's nearness is known in their midst. Near to God as he
is, there is about him a kind of heavenly serenity; he is more than
other men sensitive to the pains and tragedies of human lives and
yet he brings to bear upon them this serenity which makes for
healing. Such are those whom we commemorate so thankfully
to-day. The world around us is apathetic, for while people in
general admire goodness they feel awkward with words like saint
or saintliness. Yet it is saintliness that is able to pierce the worldly
heart or mind. It too is the authentic proof of the supernatural
claim of our Christian faith, and it keeps the Church on earth
directed towards its heavenly goal: "His servants shall serve him,
and they shall see his face."

Is there a lesson which our Church needs more vividly than the lesson of All Saints Day? We have superabundant activity, and the restless whirl of doing this and doing that. It is so in England, and it is no less so here in America. But a Church can be never so energetic, never so efficient, never so full of virtue, and yet the touch of the supernatural may be far to seek. Called to be saints! The first step is the primary one of communion with God himself; the readiness to go apart in quietness, waiting upon God: "Be still and know that I am God." "O God thou art my God, early will I seek thee." The next step, which follows, is penitence; for the authentic sense of God's presence leads quickly to that grief at the sight of ourselves beside him. Our contrition and confession of sinfulness means that amidst all our busyness in serving God we are ready to pause and to let him serve us in the absolving of those things in us which he hates to see. Would that among all of us, clergy and laity alike, these needs had larger place: the practice of retreat and withdrawal to wait upon God in stillness, and the practice of confessing our sins with care and cost. It is for the fulfilment of the Church's mission in the world that these needs are urgent. The Church must indeed be deeply involved with the present age, studying it, learning its techniques, sensitive to its aspirations and its fears; and yet as a Church we shall grapple with the present age best if there is in our Church life that other-worldly strain of which All Saints Day is the reminder. We best do God's will now if there is in us the longing for God for God's own sake which sees our present tasks in the light of our heavenly goal, where "his servants shall serve him, and they shall see his face".

To-day, a Bishop of Washington, elected and consecrated, enters upon his throne. He succeeds a man greatly loved for his goodness and his wisdom, a man known and respected far beyond the American portion of our world-wide Communion. The new Bishop brings to his task a ripe pastoral experience with the trust and gratitude of those to whom his pastoral ministry has meant so much; and the prayers of thousands surround him as he enters his high office in the Church of God.

The bishop is the shepherd, the teacher, the intercessor amidst the flock of Christ. He has before him the pattern of our Lord himself. He sees day by day Jesus the Good Shepherd who gave his life for his flock, Jesus the bringer of divine truth who says, "Everyone that is of the truth hears my voice", Jesus who on earth was found a great while before day praying in a desert place apart and now lives for ever to make intercession for us. As shepherd, the bishop finds it his joyful duty to care especially for the clergy in their care for the parishes and to bring the means of grace to the people in his own sacramental acts. As teacher, the bishop will not necessarily be a man of speculation and research, but one who brings home with clarity and conviction the faith of the scriptures and the creeds. As intercessor, he is one who goes apart with God on behalf of the people. Aaron entered the Holy of Holies with the names of the twelve tribes engraved upon his breastplate; so the bishop lifts his heart to God with the needs, the sins, and the sorrows of his people graven upon it. Thus does he set before him Christ—shepherd, teacher, priest.

As he leads and directs his diocese in the strategy of the holy war the bishop is aware of the urgent issues of the day. What problems of the world hit the Christian conscience now? There is the problem of race. Here the Church stands without compromise against every form of apartheid; races must be seen worshipping side by side, for to exclude a man of another race from the house of God is to exclude Christ. There is the problem of peace; and Christians throw the weight of their prayer and influence for the will of nations to agree to disarm and so give peace a chance. There is the problem of the terrible contrast between nations that are prosperous and nations that are in dire poverty; and the rich must urgently come to the aid of the poor. There is the problem of affluence. It is time that we in England and America paid heed to our Lord's warning against riches, and to the first beatitude, "Blessed are the poor in spirit". Ought not the life of Christians to be marked by a greater simplicity, a greater indifference to luxury and comfort? The Church's witness owes much, and will owe much again, to those who are called to the way of total simplicity, in poverty, chastity, and obedience, as monks, nuns, and friars. The otherworldly part of the Church's witness enables it to engage itself with the world's practical problems with clearer vision and swifter mobility in the contemporary scene.

"Called to be saints." It is in the vision of that calling that to-night a new bishop summons the clergy and the people to the tasks before them. By keeping that vision before himself he will, all unselfconsciously, help the clergy and the people to keep the same vision before themselves. St Thomas à Kempis said that the man of faith has two eyes; with his left eye he sees the things of earth, and with his right eye he sees the things of heaven. Let Christian people keep both eyes open and alert; and we shall see the things of earth without alarm, without distorted sight, as we look towards heaven and the saints of God, knowing that "his servants shall serve him and they shall see his face".

Whose Hearts
God Has Touched

There went with him a band of men
whose hearts God had touched.

1 Sam. 10.26

These words describe how many centuries ago there was the first choice of a man to be King in Israel; it was a task beyond all human strength, and many in the land were sure to be hostile and estranged. But he was not alone, there went with him a band of men who had felt the touch of God. It made all the difference. Do not these words come true to-day, as words can do across the lapse of centuries? To-day a man enters his task as the chief shepherd of a great portion of the Christian Church; it is a task beyond all human strength, and many in the country are not so much hostile as indifferent and aloof. But he sets out not alone; there goes with him the great band of those hearts God has touched with the faith of Christ.

We call to-day's ceremony an enthronement. What does that mean? It is the putting of a man into the seat of a ruler, for in Christ's name he will rule in the Church of God, not indeed as lording over it, but as serving it; for, under Christ, authority and humility must always go together. It is also the putting of a man into the chair of a teacher—let that not be forgotten—for a bishop is the shepherd of the people as being also the teacher of God's truth, proclaiming the truth of God's majesty, God's compassion, God's claim upon all men, and God's wonderful gift of himself to them in Christ. To shepherd and to teach, in the service of Christ, himself the good shepherd and himself the truth; to this

165

there is called one more man, the hundredth in this place, with all the frailties of human flesh and blood.

But there goes with him a band whose hearts God has touched. Is that band few or many? See the Christian Church over against the many who neglect God and forget him, and are indifferent to the truth, and this band seems small indeed. See the Christian Church across the centuries of time, with the generations of God's servants one family with us, and with the saints in heaven with us and near us, the band becomes a mighty host. Yes, the throne to which a new Archbishop steps to-day belongs not just to a generation, or a section, or a denomination. It belongs, in due succession from St Augustine, to the One, Holy, Catholic Church of Christ as first planted in this country, to a band of men and women and children whose hearts at many times and in many places God has touched; sometimes, alas, to a loyalty conventional or shallow, sometimes to an ardent faith and love, sometimes to heroic and Christ-like saintliness. Surrounded by such a cloud of witnesses, on earth and in heaven, what man who stands where I now stand could fail to gain new courage for his task?

To-day, we who by our Christian profession belong to this band of those whose heart God has touched, must needs set ourselves to much searching of mind. I speak to everyone here within Canterbury Cathedral, and to everyone who is listening or watching within their homes. I speak to all my new friends in the south, eager to get to know you and to serve you, as well as to all my old friends in the north, in Yorkshire and in Durham, on Tees-Side and on Tyne-Side too. You have to-day watched an Archbishop go to his throne: have you yourself gone with him, your own heart touched by God? Come with me, in the service of Christ: come with me, we need one another. But what does he ask of us as we go with him together? Remember, when the Bible speaks of your heart, the meaning is not only your feelings, but your will and your mind as well.

We must be sure what we have and where we stand in our own Church of England. We are a Church reformed and scriptural; let there be no doubt about that. We rejoice too in our catholic continuity, and of this the enthronement to-day is a vivid symbol. No less must we cherish that quest of intellectual freedom, that passion for truth which has marked our great thinkers and teachers, a passion never more needed than to-day when we have to present the Christian faith amid the scientific culture of our time. Scriptural, Catholic, Liberal, we shall go out from to-day pledged to every part of what, as Anglicans, we have received and need still to stir ourselves to use. But, as we go, we look more widely. Our Church must reach out in the quest of unity, for Christ is longing that there will go with him not separated bands of followers, but, as one band, all those whose heart God has touched.

Here in England the Church and the State are linked together, and we use that link in serving the community. But, in that service and in rendering to God the things that are God's we ask for a greater freedom in the ordering and in the urgent revising of our forms of worship. If the link of Church and State were broken, it would not be we who ask for this freedom who broke it, but those—if there be such—who denied that freedom to us.

Yet all the time there is, for us whose hearts God has touched, the supreme task to bring home to the people God himself, in his majesty, his compassion, his claim upon mankind, his astounding gift of his very self in Jesus, the Word-made-flesh. We cannot fulfil the task for this country unless we are striving to fulfil it towards the whole of the world. It therefore demands the service of men and women who will go anywhere in the world in Christ's obedience, who will witness to Christ's love in the insistence that races, black and white, are brothers together of equal worth. Here at home our mission means for the Church a constant involvement in the community; we shall strive to penetrate the world of industry, of science, of art and literature, of sight and sound, and in this penetration we must approach as learners as well as teachers. We need to be learning not only many new techniques, but also what God is saying to us through the new and exciting circumstances of our time. Yet, because it is God to whom we witness, we need no less a constant detachment, a will to go apart and wait upon God in quiet, in silence, lest by our very busyness we should rob ourselves and rob others of the realization of God's presence: "Be *still*, and know that I am God." Would that everyone whose heart God has once touched would guard times of quietness amid our noisy, bustling life, to let God touch the heart again. Is there a more urgent need than this for every layman, every priest or bishop or archbishop in our Church?

Let me leave with you some words of two Christian writers of old time. Here are words of a Greek Christian; his name was Irenaeus. "Offer thy heart to God in a soft and tractable state, lest thou lose the impress of his fingers; lest by being hardened thou might miss both his craftsmanship and thy life." But how may we do this, so fond we are of our wilfulness and our pride? Here are words of a Latin Christian, Augustine, not of Canterbury, but of Hippo in Africa. He prayed, "Lord, take my heart from me, for I cannot give it thee. Keep it for thyself, for I cannot keep it for thee; and save me in spite of myself."

If that be my own prayer to-day, "Lord, take my heart from me, keep it for thyself", will you, as you come with me, make it your prayer, for me and for yourself? We must help one another, and serve one another, both in our family of the Church of England and in Christendom near and far. Help one another, serve one another, for the times are urgent and the days are evil. Help one another, serve one another, as from this hundredth ceremony at St Augustine's throne there goes a band of those whose heart God has touched.